Golfers have a sta[...]
goes first: 'I learn[...]
can watch anothe[...]
by watching how [...]
has allowed all of us to 'learn on her ball.' This is an
incredible story of pain and suffering. But more than
that, it is a story of God's absolute faithfulness in a very
dark place. You'll be inspired by this book and when
and if you have to go to your own dark place, you will
be thankful that you had an pooortunity to 'learn on the
ball' of Margaret Lamkin.

Steve Brown,
President of Key LifeNetwork, Inc.

This is more than a compelling story. It is chock-full of
life lessons that teach us more about our Sovereign God.
Margaret learned these lessons well, and she shares them
with us in a spirit of gratitude and humility.

Susan Hunt
Head of WIC of PCA

At one point or another all of us face trials in life that
challenge our faith. Margaret Lamkin is warm and honest
as she shares about her faith in Christ during her struggle
with a life-threatening ordeal. We can all find hope and
inspiration in the pages of Margaret's story.

Richard Pratt,
Reformed Theological Seminary, Orlando

It is my great privilege to have known Margaret since
she was a student/teacher for InterVarsity Christian
Fellowship at Davidson College. Since I was aware of
her effective ministry, my first prayer, when I received
the note requesting prayer during the severe trauma that

she went through with her surgery and post-operative recovery, was, "Lord, why?" This book tells you why. God makes no mistakes. His Divine Providence is sometimes challenging to fathom but always sure and unerring. It is for His glory that we endure – and in our endurance others may see Jesus Christ in us. See Christ at work in Margaret through the pages of this book and join her in giving God the glory and honor.

Harry L. Reeder III
Senior Pastor, Briarwood Presbyterian Church

My Flesh and My Heart May Fail

A Personal Testimony of Open Heart Surgery

Margaret Carroll Lamkin

Christian Focus

Christian Focus Publications publishes biblically-accurate books for adults and children. The books in the adult range are published in three imprints.

Christian Heritage contains classic writings from the past.

Christian Focus contains popular works including biographies, commentaries, doctrine, and Christian living.

Mentor focuses on books written at a level suitable for Bible College and seminary students, pastors, and others; the imprint includes commentaries, doctrinal studies, examination of current issues, and church history.

For a free catalogue of all our titles, please write to
Christian Focus Publications,
Geanies House, Fearn,
Ross-shire, IV20 1TW, Great Britain

For details of our titles visit us on our web site
http://www.christianfocus.com

© Margaret Carroll Lamkin
ISBN 1 85792 643 9

Published in 2001
by Christian Focus Publications,
Geanies House, fearn, Ross-shire,
IV20 1TW, Great Britain

Cover design by Owen Daily

Scripture references are from the New International Version, published by Hodder and Stoughton, London

Contents

Acknowledgments

Dedicated to the Lord for His glory, Mom and Dad and my brother, William, for staying with me through this long trial. Thanks to Dr. James Kirklin for using the talent God has given him to perform open heart surgeries, to Trinity Presbyterian Church in Montgomery, Alabama; Trinity Presbyterian Church in Tuscaloosa, Alabama; Eastwood Presbyterian Church in Montgomery, Alabama; Shearer Presbyterian, South Lake Presbyterian Church, and Tabernacle ARP Churches in North Carolina – and to everyone else who has lifted a prayer on my behalf.

Dedicated to my loving husband, Bill Lamkin, who shows unconditional love to me in spite of my physical limitations. I am thankful for his patience throughout this project as I hid out with the computer for weeks and months while finishing this book. My life would not be nearly as rich and full without his compassion as we minister together.

Also dedicated to Sandy Ford (1960-1981) whose life story encouraged me to live each day as unto the Lord (before I even knew I would have heart surgery). To Sandy, whom I am excited to meet and hang out with in heaven.

FOREWORD

Os Guinness subtitles his book, *God in the Dark,* 'The Assurance of Faith Beyond a Shadow of Doubt.' He points out that Christian thinking, Christian choices, Christian action do not bring life into believers; they are expressions of the life that is already there.

Margaret Carroll Lamkin has given us a provocative testimony concerning the life given us by Christ, new and eternal, designed to be proactively applied at every juncture of our earthly pilgrimage. This small volume paints an exceedingly large and uplifting portrait of how one may develop an assured faith in the midst of painful struggles with potent memories of hurt and insecurity, in the crucible of enormous physical debilitation and stress.

I became pastor of Trinity Presbyterian Church in Montgomery, Alabama, early in 1988. Margaret was then in her first year at my own collegiate alma mater, Davidson College. Thus, when she came home on breaks from school, we had much to talk about and share. This included how we were, or were not, growing in the Lord. Such conversations, happily for me, have continued across the years.

As Margaret's pastor, I was both witness and

involved participant in the events recorded in this book, through which the living God transformed not only Margaret, but also all of us who knew and loved her, along with scores of people brought into her life during those momentous and faith-shaping times.

My conviction is that, through their encounter with *My Flesh and My Heart May Fail*, readers will be gripped by the humility, integrity and transparency of a young woman given over to God. This, in turn, will compel us to examine our own relationship with Him, and in that scrutiny to determine whether the life of Christ is really in us, and, if so, to what extent that life enables us to deal with issues of living and dying.

Oswald Chambers, in *My Utmost for His Highest*, has pointed counsel for us all: 'Be ruthless with yourself if you are given to talking about the experiences you have had. Faith that is sure of itself is not faith. Faith that is sure of God is the only faith there is.' Thank you, Margaret, for demonstrating just such a faith, thus blessing and encouraging everyone who reads your story. Soli Deo Gloria!

Cortez A. Cooper, Jr.

Introduction

As I write these words, I am at University of Alabama at Birmingham Hospital, where I have been for almost five weeks. I am twenty-three years old. I tell my story to encourage people of all ages who encounter difficult circumstances. Know that God receives all the honor and glory because He brought me out of the Valley of the Shadow of Death. My allergic reaction to the bypass machine during surgery (which caused additional complications) was a one in 50,000 possibility. God knew that I would have this reaction; He is sovereign; He accomplishes His divine plan through what appears in human eyes to be foolish. May this testimony tell of God's love and grace. May this creation be a testimony of His faithfulness whether I live ten more years or ten more days. May one soul come to know Christ through my trial or through a friend who knew about it. In any case, He remains.

10-22-92

When I wrote the above words, I really did not expect this book would develop a life of its own. *My Flesh and My Heart May Fail* tells the story of my life and, more importantly, details God's hand in all things. Each 'autobiographical' chapter is followed by a 'truth' chapter. While this format may not always chronologically unfold, each section reveals a biblical principle I learned.

1

A Heart Not Right

Most children do not like going to the doctor or the dentist. Neither did I! Even as an adult, I do not enjoy anyone inflicting pain on me. As a child, however, my favorite doctor was Dr. L. N. Bargeron, Pediatric Cardiologist at The University of Alabama at Birmingham Hospital (UAB). The University of Alabama at Birmingham Hospital is a teaching and research hospital located in the center of Alabama. It was the first hospital in Alabama to perform open heart surgery, and it still has a renowned cardiology department.

I started seeing Dr. Bargeron when I was about two years old after my pediatrician in Montgomery, Alabama, Dr. Hugh Frazer, detected a 'murmur' in my heart and decided to send me to the nearest pediatric cardiology specialist. Of course, I do not remember much about first visiting Dr. Bargeron since I was so young. I continued to have check-ups with Dr. Bargeron annually or biannually, and as I grew older he became my favorite doctor. I was used to getting allergy shots regularly, having my finger pricked for blood, taking strep tests and other 'less than pleasant' activities associated with doctor visits. But visits to Dr. Bargeron were fabulous! There was no pain involved with the visits, which consisted of an xray and an EKG. In addition, the office was filled with toys and fairly healthy looking children.

Yet one of the best things about seeing Dr. Bargeron was being able to miss school. After the appointments, I ate lollipops and spent the day in Birmingham, which included eating lunch and shopping with my mother. As I became a teenager, I looked forward to these trips because I could pick out new school clothes at Brookwood Mall, a larger mall than those in Montgomery. For lunch after my appointment, my mother and I would sometimes walk to Waits' Cafe, a wonderful bakery and deli, or we would go to the Magic Pan and eat crepes for lunch. Neither of these restaurants exists in Birmingham any more, so I look back with nostalgia on those days!

Dr. Bargeron suspected that my aortic valve was a bicuspid valve (consisting of two flaps of skin coming together) rather than a tricuspid (three-pronged) one. He encouraged me to do whatever I wanted as far as exercise and having a normal childhood; however, his instructions were, 'Don't run track and don't overdo it.' On several occasions, when I questioned him, Dr. Bargeron said that I was doing fine but that one day (when I turned twenty or thirty, which seemed light years away), I might have to have the valve replaced. He continued to watch the 'murmur' and to make sure that the heart was not growing larger as a result of the valve's insufficiency.

Encountering no drastic effects or obvious signs of this diagnosis, I ran relay races, participated in Physical Education (PE) classes at school, swam almost every day of the summers and maintained an active childhood. However, I did not enjoy PE or organized activities because I was not good at them. I was a very slow runner and usually the last one picked for relays! My heart's abnormality caused blood to flow backward every time it pumped. Therefore, I had to exert more energy and became fatigued quickly. Surprisingly, I developed an interest in basketball in late elementary and junior high school (probably because I was rebelling against my mother's desire for me to be a ballerina!). Although my shooting was fairly accurate, I was, again, too slow. After trying out for the varsity team for two years previously, I finally made it in the ninth and tenth grades. Most of the time I kept the bench very cosy, but I found a sport that I enjoyed and one in which most girls did not participate.

Sometimes my interests developed not from skill but as a result of attention seeking. I especially wanted to get a reaction from my mother. For instance, I was very stubborn as a child and would decide not to do something just because an authority figure wanted me to! I believe that Dr. James Dobson may have written *The Strong-Willed Child* using me as the paradigm and case study! Although I hate to admit it, I was very selfish and deceitful as a youngster. I enjoyed making fun of people and putting others down so that I could have my way. While my family attended a local church, I do not think that any of us had a personal relationship with the Lord Jesus Christ until years later when we began attending a Bible-believing church. Because my parents thought I was old enough, I went through the Communicant's Class in the fifth grade, even though I did not comprehend the seriousness of the membership vows I took to join the church. I did not really understand the Communicant's Class, but I participated in it nonetheless. I assumed that I was a Christian because I lived in America and was not of another faith. In addition, I believed in God; I just did not know Him personally.

Thankfully, my parents joined Trinity Presbyterian Church in America (PCA) about two years later. This church was (and still is) a vibrant, Biblically based church. Many Christians I met at Trinity had a joy that transcended the happiness of their circumstances. For some reason, I often felt angry and unhappy. I acted bad even when I was trying to 'be good'. I used to have the nickname 'me firsty' around home because I only looked out for my personal interests, and my selfishness was obvious even when I was a young child.

After we joined this church, I really began to see that individual lives were impacted by God and His Word. I saw that Christians had something that I wanted. Attending and eventually joining Trinity Church, I felt as if I was desperately missing 'something'. Yet I was not aware of what that 'something' was. For the first time I heard that I was sinful and going to spend eternity in hell unless I accepted Jesus as my Savior. My heart began to be receptive to the gospel of grace.

It was not difficult to convince me that I was (and still am) a sinner, and I began to understand that Jesus paid the penalty for my sin on the cross. When I was in seventh grade, I accepted Him as my Lord and Savior.

After becoming a Christian, I loved attending church, youth group and choir. Looking back now, I probably went 'overboard' and became legalistic (dare I say pharisaic?). My new relationship with God led me to look down on others who did not 'do' as I thought they should.

This ugly attitude, which I thought was right at the time, cost me a lot. I became a 'goody-two-shoes' at school, and I began removing myself from former friends. At our small, private school, The Montgomery Academy, a lot of people attended church but did not live as Christians. Rather than loving individuals there, I presented an attitude of disapproval.

Still, I believe that being in the world but not 'of the world' is one of the most difficult areas in the Christian life. As a teenager, on weekends I became involved with more activities with youth group friends. Actually, there were very few Montgomery Academy students who were in our youth group. As a result of my spending more time with church friends, I hurt some people with whom I had been to school since kindergarten. I saw the youth group as a haven from phony 'Christians'.

I was hungry to grow and to learn about God and His Word. One of the most memorable ways I began to grow and learn was through youth choir tours. I had the opportunity to go on three summer choir tours with our Trinity Joysingers Youth Choir. Traveling to other parts of the United States, meeting children whose lifestyles were different from ours, memorizing the music, teaching Vacation Bible Schools (VBS), going door to door inviting children to VBS, and working together as a team were all fabulous preparations for life and growth in Christ.

The summer after I finished eighth grade we went to the Navajo Indian Reservation in New Mexico. The choir tour lasted about two weeks. We performed choir concerts in churches on the way to New Mexico, stayed there for one week and did VBS for three different groups, each in a different location on the reservation. We then sang and did a little sightseeing on the way home. We spent one day in Silverton and Durango, Colorado and actually had a snowball fight in June on one of the mountains. We took trips to Window Rock and to Canyon DeShay and once ate authentic Navajo food. While we were in Tucumcari, New Mexico, we were caught in a tornado or wind storm, and even now those who were on the trip tell stories about events that happened as the power went off at the hotel. One of the girls, Tina, sprained her ankle and came to our room to lie down. While in our room, Tina dropped her gum in the bed of my roommate. Meanwhile, in the middle of the night, after Tina had left our room, my friend's underwear stuck to the bed! My roommate began to shout: 'My underwear is stuck to the bed!' We were silly eighth grade girls, laughing and fumbling around in the dark trying to remove our friend from her sticky predicament.

The next two summers our choir went to Boston and then to Philadelphia, employing similar travel and VBS formats. On these trips we visited Washington DC, Ogunquit, Maine, an Amish community, and other interesting sights. Mr. Bob Woodham, our choir director, encouraged us to work hard and then rewarded us by taking us to these adventurous places.

In addition to these choir tours, several members of our youth group went to Coral Ridge Presbyterian Church in Fort Lauderdale, Florida, to be trained in Evangelism Explosion during spring break of my tenth-grade year. We met youth from Coral Ridge and partnered with them in going to the beach and presenting the gospel to individuals we met. Ending this fantastic learning experience, we went to Disney World before returning home.

So during my teenage years, I was growing and learning about being a Christian and ministering to others, even though I was struggling with the cliques and nominal Christianity at school. Several of us started a faculty/student prayer group that met before school in one of the classrooms. I tried, as best as I knew how, to be an example, to reach out to 'misfits' and to grow in Christ.

As for my heart condition, I do not know how to describe my childhood with this abnormality, mostly because I was unaware that I was any different from other children or adults. For this, I am thankful. While I knew that I did not have as much energy as others, I did not understand the potential seriousness of my condition. Sometimes when I was the last one chosen for a relay race or exhausted after a long basketball practice, I tried not to complain and not to draw attention to myself. But I often wished that I could tell others what it was like to have a fear of surgery in the back of my mind. Thus, certain aspects of my childhood were normal. Other events were supernatural.

Since I had already become a Christian by the time I finally made the varsity girls basketball team at our school, the promise I relied upon regularly during basketball season and other tiring activities was Isaiah 40:29-31: 'Those who wait on the LORD shall renew their strength. They shall mount up like eagles with wings of great length. They shall run and not grow weary. They shall walk and not faint. He gives strength to the weary and power to the saints.' God gave me the strength to run 'suicide' drills at the end of practice and to maintain a fairly active childhood. Thankfully, at an early age, I knew that a day would come when I would be strong and swift in a perfect body for eternity.

2

A Heart's Strength

As I grew older and began to understand my heart problem, I believed that my condition was unique. None of my friends made annual visits to cardiologists. As a matter of fact, I thought I was the only one alive with a misformed aortic valve. However, I began to understand that my aortic valve insufficiency was not uncommon. I also learned that my spiritual heart's corruption was not unique but universal. The Lord began revealing my inner sin and selfishness as an early teenager. To further understand my inner heart's condition, we must look at Genesis.

As my family became active in Trinity Presbyterian Church, I started to hear the word 'sin'. Through youth group, Sunday school and Fellowship of Christian Athletes, God began showing me that all individuals have sinful hearts. And sin first entered the world when Adam and Eve were created. Genesis 1:1 recounts creation: 'In the beginning God created the heavens and the earth.' Before God spoke creation into being, there was nothing. By His spoken word alone, everything we know of this life came into existence. In addition, He made Adam and Eve in His image. Of all the animals, plants, waters and land, God looked at what He had made and saw that it was good. But man was the crown of creation according to Genesis 1:26: 'Then God said, "Let us make man in our image, in our likeness, and let them rule over the fish of the sea and the birds of the air, over the livestock, over all the earth. . ."' As God looked over the finality of His work, He saw that it was 'very good.' *The Heidelberg Catechism* asks, 'Did God create man evil and perverse like this? No. On the contrary, God created man good and in His image, that is, in true righteousness and holiness, so that he might rightly know God his Creator, love Him with his whole heart, and live with Him in eternal blessedness, praising and glorifying Him' (Q6). Adam and Eve enjoyed perfect communion and fellowship with the Lord.

However, Satan entered the Garden in the form of a serpent and tempted Eve. She disobeyed God; Adam followed. The one tree from which Adam and Eve were not to partake, the tree of the knowledge of good and evil, was the one Satan used to tempt them. Although Adam and Eve had full reign over the entire Garden with that one exception, they succumbed and disobeyed God. Because of their disobedience, everyone born since Adam and Eve is born in sin and corrupted by sin. 'Did our first parents continue in the estate wherein they were created? Our first parents, being left to the freedom of their own will, fell from the estate wherein they were created' (*The Westminster Shorter Catechism* Q13). This Fall corrupted the entirety of the human race – now all people are born in and plagued with sin.

As Romans 5:12 explains, 'Therefore, just as sin entered the world through one man, and death through sin, and in this way death came to all men, because all sinned.' When we are born, we are not innocent, blank slates, upon which our environment writes our personalities, likes, dislikes and character. Rather, we are born enemies of God. If left to our own devices, we hate God and seek our own gain. It is not just our actions that are evil; but our thoughts, motives and pride are depraved. God's standard is perfection, perfect obedience to all of His commandments. Therefore, we 'all have sinned and fall short of the glory of God' (Rom. 3:23). 'But are we so perverted that we are altogether unable to do good and prone to do evil? Yes, unless we are born again through the Spirit of God' (*The Heidelberg Catechism* Q8). Everything about us, all that makes us who we are, is infested by this disease of sin.

Thankfully, God first began heart transplant surgery, removing sinful hearts and replacing them with righteous ones. In Ezekiel 36:26 the

Lord says: 'I will give you a new heart and put a new spirit in you; I will remove from you your heart of stone and give you a heart of flesh.' Because of our sin, our hearts are like cold stones before God. We are by nature enemies of God. But because of His mercy, God restores us to life. He performs transplants on His children, removing the stones and giving us fleshly hearts. We gain breath and life eternal through this operation.

Through Jesus Christ we are given these new hearts. Jesus is the only remedy for our condition. Because God's standard is perfect obedience to all of His requirements, Jesus is the only One who could keep them (since He is God). No one else, not even what we might refer to as 'a good person', can perfectly keep all of God's law. Paul tells of Christ's sacrifice on our behalf: '[he] did not consider equality with God something to be grasped, but made himself nothing, taking the very nature of a servant, being made in human likeness. And being found in appearance as a man, he humbled himself and became obedient to death – even death on a cross!' (Phil. 2:6-8). Christ left the glory of heaven to become man (thus being both fully man and fully God), to walk among us, see our hurts, pains and condition and to be the only propitiation for the punishment we deserve.

In order to be restored to a right relationship

with God, we must acknowledge our sin and our need for a Savior and trust in Jesus as our only hope. 'Did God leave all mankind to perish in the estate of sin and misery? God having, out of his mere good pleasure, from all eternity, elected some to everlasting life, did enter into a covenant of grace to deliver them out of an estate of sin and misery and to bring them into an estate of salvation by a Redeemer' (*The Westminster Shorter Catechism* Q 20). Those who trust in Christ's finished work on the Cross are no longer seen by God as enemies but received as righteous children.

As a teenager, I started to understand my position as a sinner before a holy God. In 1985, I wrote these words:

I see the girl across the room, how rude she can be
Sometimes selfish, sometimes angry, tearing others
down –
How familiar she looks to me, yet I cannot quite
recall the face.
All I see is sin inside and the fear of giving love
Because hurt might accompany it.
As she looks me in the eye, I see, even more, the
resemblance –
For she is my own reflection.

Never did I doubt that I was sinful and selfish – that fact was clear and obvious to me. However,

I fought with surrendering my life to Christ, not wanting to 'give up' my ways and my will. At times I tried to argue intellectually against the premises of Christianity. I wanted to believe in God yet live as I pleased. Ultimately, I could not resist God's calling me to Himself. I realized that a relationship with Christ was 'all or nothing'. I could not just separate my life like shoe boxes in the top of my closet – one for Sunday, one for school, one for dating, one for friends, etc. I recognized that my entire being was corrupted by sin and that my entire being needed a Redeemer. My restoration with God may be described by the words of a marvelous, old pilgrim hymn:

'I sought the Lord and afterward I knew
He moved my soul to seek Him, seeking me;
It was not that I found, O Savior true;
No, I was found of Thee.
Thou didst reach forth Thy hand and mine enfold;
I walked and sank not on the storm-vexed sea;
'Twas not so much that I on Thee took hold
As Thou, dear Lord, on me.
I find, I walk, I love, but O the whole
Of love is but my answer, Lord, to Thee!
For Thou wert long beforehand with my soul;
Always Thou lovedst me.'[1]

Since sin had affected the entirety of my being, not just my actions or words, I could only find freedom, forgiveness, joy and true life when Jesus Christ became the Lord over all of my life. Everything had to be under His direction and guidance.

Even after I received the free gift of eternal life through faith in Jesus, I still struggled with sins such as rebellion against my parents, gossip, hateful words and thoughts. I began learning more about sanctification, the process wherein God continues to mould us and make us more like His Son. Nowhere does God promise an easy road to righteousness. Our Lord does assure us that while we are in these earthly bodies we will grow and struggle. Eventually, we will be like Him, completely righteous, when we meet Him face to face!

Sanctification is clearly defined in *The Westminster Shorter Catechism*: 'What is sanctification? Sanctification is the work of God's free grace, whereby we are renewed in the whole man after the image of God, and are enabled more and more to die unto sin, and live unto righteousness' (Q35). God's Word is truth – if we are His, He sees us as righteous and will make us perfect when we die!

As the reader will learn, my congenital heart defect resulted in my need for a valve replacement surgery. A few weeks before the operation, I attended a Bible study where the leader asked, 'What is the heart?' The group answered by discovering that it's the central mechanism of life in the physical sense and the very core of being in the spiritual sense. All of the body's functioning depends upon the heart's; all of our actions result from inmost desires. Followers of Christ are to 'love the Lord your God with all your heart and with all your soul and with all your mind,' according to Matthew 22:37. The word 'heart' used in this verse represents all that we are. We are not to simply know about God, but our hearts are to thirst for Him.

When I was facing surgery, several people asked questions such as, 'Are you okay?' 'Do you feel sick?' 'Surely the minister was wrong when he said you were having open-heart surgery?' Because I looked fine on the outside and could do what most people could, many thought I did not need surgery.

I was also surprised to discover that I needed a new aortic valve! About six months before my cardiology appointment, I had been for a regular physical. I remember feeling tired, maybe having a sore throat. At that time my doctor gave me some potent multivitamins and told me that I was anaemic. Meanwhile, my heart was becoming enlarged. I knew that I was unusually tired, but only a specialized test would detect that my heart's left ventricle was enlarged and that the aortic valve was functioning poorly.

Our lives are often similar to my weakening heart: onlookers never know that we are falling apart inside. Throughout my life, I have been able to detect people who appear fine but are struggling inside. Most people pass through their day exchanging pleasantries such as, 'Hey! How are you?' 'Oh, I'm fine,' or 'I'm great,' or 'I'm really busy!' Sometimes individuals respond to hellos and similar greetings with statements such as 'I'm fantastic!' These same individuals sometimes are feeling horribly lonely but refuse to admit that they are hurting. 1 Samuel 16:7 summarizes the whole inner heart condition: 'The LORD does not look at the things man looks at. Man looks at the outward appearance, but the LORD looks at the heart.' We can fool some people sometimes, but we can never fool God. Accepting Christ as the Lord of my life, the only hope for salvation, and the only cure for my spiritual heart disease gives me hope that will endure when this life is over.

Ten days before my scheduled surgery in 1992, I sent a postcard to an older man in my church who was having tests and cancer treatment at Oschner Medical Clinic. In this note, I told him that I had been praying for him that week. I wrote: 'My surgery will be on August 21. A verse I've claimed during this time is Psalm 73:26, "My flesh and my heart may fail, but God is the strength of my heart and my portion forever."' As believers, we can truly know that God is our strength. When heaven and earth pass away, our stuff, our accolades or earthly things we have hoped in will vanish. Although I had no idea that my heart would fail during surgery or that my resulting diagnosis would be congestive heart failure, I was trusting that Christ was my strength and salvation. Even now, I am resting on Him.

3

Off to College

In the fall of 1987, I packed my belongings and headed for Davidson College after graduation from high school. I had been to Davidson's July Experience the previous summer, a program for around ninety upcoming high school seniors. We stayed in the dorms during the month of July, took two mini courses and participated in numerous planned activities. It was my first exposure to flag football and Davidson's lake campus. Since I enjoyed July Experience, I decided to apply 'early decision' to Davidson. And after being accepted, I enrolled and joined to graduate in 1991. Of course, in my freshman year I picked up the 'freshman fifteen' (pounds) and decided to start exercising regularly to keep off the weight.

My next visit with Dr. Bargeron was the first summer after beginning college. He asked about my activity level and told me to continue doing what I felt like doing. His only order was, 'Do not overdo!' He said that if I got tired, I had to stop. However, he also said, 'If a cute guy asks you to play football or to go jogging, then go – just don't push yourself for exercise.' I cannot say with 100 % honesty that I only waited for cute guys to ask me before doing any exercise. If I had waited, I may not have exercised since that day! Most of the time, I would stop when I was tired – but I had a difficult time measuring tiredness.

During my freshman year, my roommate Sally and I did aerobics in our room and encouraged one another to exercise. While at Davidson, I continued to play basketball at the intramural level. We did not have a varsity ladies team at that time, but several of us began developing a club team which eventually became a varsity team after we graduated. Our club team practiced several nights a week and played other area college club teams. I enjoyed playing for the fun and excitement of the sport without the pressures of tough practices and efforts to please the coach! Everyone played, and my team won the intramural basketball championship several years.

I used my 'free time' (whatever free time a Davidson student has) to become involved with InterVarsity Christian Fellowship and Shearer Presbyterian Church in nearby Mooresville, while belonging to Rusk House, and all-female eating hall and social club. In addition, I served as a reporter for *The Davidsonian* (our student-run newspaper) and the 'Mecklenburg Neighbors' section of *The Charlotte Observer* and participated in several campus events and committees.

During this time, I struggled not with my heart condition, but with my identity. I entered Davidson from The Montgomery Academy, a small private school, which I had attended since kindergarten. Many times those thirteen years felt very socially restricting. Students at Montgomery Academy had known each other since birth (literally), and peer pressure and conformity seemed the norm. Arriving at Davidson, I found a lot of students who wanted to be different. Many were individualists.

Through my involvement in campus life, I continually saw the truth that only two things from this life remain: God's Word and individuals' souls. I spent the entire first year thinking that I was the only conservative Christian on campus. Finding others whose theological beliefs were similar to mine was difficult; many times I felt lonely and confused. Having previously enjoyed a wonderful, active youth group and youth choir, suddenly I was surrounded by people who did not believe that Scripture was God's divinely inspired Word. I faced a two-year Humanities course in which several professors believed Genesis to be just another 'creation myth' and did not see the Bible as historically accurate, literal or without error. It was hard to find a true 'soul-mate,' someone, like me, who held the conviction that the Scripture is the only rule given by God to instruct how we may glorify and enjoy Him forever.

A turning point in my life occurred after spring break of my first year at Davidson. First, I realized that I was not the only Christian on campus. Secondly, I knew that if I felt alone (as an evangelical Christian), others must feel isolated too. I did not have to go overseas or live in a hut with Indians to be a missionary; everywhere I walked I was called to be a 'Truth Bearer.' And we definitely need truth bearers in these agnostic and apathetic places – college campuses. I began praying that God would place people in my path that were lonely and struggling, and He did. A girl who lived on my hall learned that her uncle had died. She was crying in the janitorial closet, and we sat together for hours as she wept. Another day I entered my room and heard hysterical crying next door. I knocked on the door, and my hall-mate needed a hug and someone to listen to her.

Each year God provided me with more Christian friends and more opportunities to minister to hurting individuals. After my freshman year, I went on a short-term summer mission trip to Gyzcko, Poland, with four other members of my home church. This trip was not only eye-opening, as Poland was still a communist country, but also it was refreshing and encouraging. While in Poland, I was challenged by the team leader to return to Davidson and to be involved in reaching students and discipling others. I wrote a letter to friends and family members whom I knew were praying for me throughout these college years. The letter, written in September 1988, read as follows:

Dear Friends and Family:
Although I am no longer in Poland, I am in a mission field nonetheless. Yes, you guessed it – I am back at Davidson! I know now that going to Poland and sharing the Gospel there was simply preparation for what I would encounter here for the next nine months.

I would like to share with you some of the ways in which the Lord has answered my prayers and blessed me so far. I met a guy on the Poland trip whose friend, Tom, is a sophomore at Davidson and is a member of Perimeter PCA in Atlanta. Anyway, Jim, the Poland friend, told me that Tom had been really distressed with Davidson last year and that he did not have any close Christian fellowship here. So, when I got here I called Tom who said, 'Margaret, it's so funny that you called because my roommate Bill and I were just talking about how we are going to really share with and reach out to others.'

Well, the story gets even better. I met with both Tom and Bill and we went to Charlotte to worship at Christ Covenant PCA and talked a lot about how we want to be accountable to each other, build each other up and be a support for each other. We realize that God has brought us all together with the same convictions for His purpose.

Then I began to pray for some Christians to disciple and encourage in the faith. As it turns out, a girl across the hall from me, Karen, is a Christian, growing in her faith and looking for some fellowship, also along with her boyfriend, Jack, and his roommate, Stewart. Then I met a freshman girl, Debbie, at the Chapel Committee meeting later and invited her and her roommate, Tammy, to InterVarsity. And at InterVarsity that night I saw a junior girl that I knew from last year (Amy) and began talking to her. She had been in France and Italy all summer as a missionary and had prayed that she would find fellowship at Davidson.

To top all of this off and to try and sum it up, I found a small PCA church about ten miles from here and contacted the minister, Rev. Wade Malloy, who invited me and the friends that I was bringing to church to eat lunch at his house after the service the following week. So I took Debbie, Tammy, Tom, Amy, Karen, Jack, Stewart and four others with me. During the service, Mr. Malloy extended the lunch invitation to all of the Davidson students in the congregation. Twenty-four of us stayed, and there were more than that at the service! [Wade Malloy still gives me a hard time about my ability to draw a crowd!]

As for the present, Amy and I are planning to lead a girls' Bible study; Rev. Malloy wants to teach a Sunday school/ Bible study class for all of us who are interested; I have given Karen a devotional book, and we are all praying for unity and revival here.

That's where you fit in! We need your prayers. Tom and Bill are Young Life leaders at a high school in Charlotte, and Bill is teaching a Bible study at his fraternity. Please pray for them as well as for me, Amy and the other people that I have mentioned. Please pray for Rev. Malloy at Shearer, and his ministry. Pray that I can find an older Christian 'role model' whom I can consult in times of severe stress. Also pray for InterVarsity and its ministry, that members don't appear 'holier than thou' or condescending but rather exhibitors of Christ's love . . . . So we're not going to exclude ourselves by any means, but we are going to do the opposite, that is, reach out to as many walks of life as possible. . . PRAY FOR THE DAVIDSON CAMPUS AS A WHOLE!!

As for me (Col. 2:2-3) 'My purpose is that they may be encouraged in heart and united in love, so that they may have the full riches of complete understanding, in order that they may know the mystery of God, namely, Christ, in whom are hidden all the treasures of wisdom and knowledge.'

I returned for my sophomore year, more inspired to be an effective witness and faced difficult, unexpected challenges. The previous year, my roommate Sally and I had been involved in a group called Westminster Fellowship. This group met on Sunday nights, shared a 'snack' supper, and discussed modern-day issues college students face. Initially, Sally and I went to Westminster Fellowship because it was a nice change from cafeteria food. We also enjoyed the interesting 'religious' discussions and opinions about homosexuality, ecumenicism, drinking and other topics. As I became more involved, the present leaders asked me to consider becoming a leader for the upcoming school year. The group, however, did not emphasize prayer or God's Word.

While ministering in Poland, our team leader, Russell Murray, had asked me about Christian fellowship at Davidson and challenged me upon return to become involved with an evangelical group on campus. I explained to Russell that Davidson basically had only two groups, Westminster and InterVarsity. I also told him that I did not click with the people at InterVarsity. However, he encouraged me to see if Westminster would agree to implement Scripture as the focal point of their discussions. If not, he suggested that I join InterVarsity and help change its image.

Thus, when my sophomore year began, I met with the student leaders of Westminster and provided suggestions for the group: that we actually study the Bible with a study guide, still covering various topics individuals wanted to discuss, and that we pray and emphasize prayer at each meeting. None of the other students wanted to change the format or to use the Bible, so I declined the invitation to be a leader of Westminster.

As I became less involved with Westminster Fellowship, I devoted more time to InterVarsity Christian Fellowship and became a leader the second half of my sophomore year. I enjoyed the large group meetings and our small planning times and prayer. We had wonderful retreats, hayrides, special speakers and social events.

Furthermore, InterVarsity provided a Biblical framework for students to grow in Christ, fellowship and service. And I began enjoying the people!

Several months into my second year at Davidson, I discovered I had mononucleosis. During parents' weekend, my mother came to Davidson and we stayed in the nearby hotel practically the entire weekend so that I could rest and recuperate. Several months later, my maternal grandfather passed away. And even later, I developed kidney stones, which I had never experienced before or since that year. During the kidney stone episode, my roommate had to drive me to the hospital in Charlotte, stopping frequently along the way because I needed bathroom breaks. It definitely seemed like I was being tested during my sophomore year. After I had been to Poland and returned from a mountain-top experience, the next few steps took me into another valley!

The summer after my sophomore year, I lived with my paternal grandmother in Ozark, Alabama. I could write another entire book about her life and walk with Christ! We had a wonderful time together while I worked for the local weekly newspaper, *The Southern Star*. I enjoyed the opportunity of entering into 'Mema's' life, eating lunch with ladies from her Widow's Club and attending church and community events together. She was the chairman of her church's visitation to elderly and shut-ins, and she was eighty at that time! Since that time, 'Mema' has gone to be with the Lord, but I will always treasure my summer in Ozark as one of refreshment and renewal before returning to Davidson.

As I returned for my junior year, I had been selected by faculty, staff and students to be a Hall Counselor. In this position, I was responsible (along with another Hall Counselor) for thirty freshman ladies and their adjustment to college life. We returned to campus early for training, and during the first few weeks we were busy setting up hall swaps (with freshman male halls), having the freshman cake race, regatta and games at the lake campus, and assigning our students to faculty advisors. While the year started with a bang, reality hit a few weeks later.

One of the most dramatic events that occurred during my time at Davidson was Hurricane Hugo. This powerful storm was expected to lose its power before coming inland; however, it hit Davidson's campus around 2–3 a.m. one Thursday night in September. In the middle of the night, we heard trees crashing and winds that sounded as if they could blow the entire dorm into pieces. We all sat out in the hallway, some of the students holding teddy bears and blankets, and waited until the storm was over. Early the next morning, all of the power was out in the town and on campus. One of the faculty members, Dr. Randy Nelson, who was also a Freshman Advisor for students on my hall, walked from his home over to Richardson Dorm, the freshman ladies' dorm, at around 7 a.m. to make sure that we were okay, offering to help with the clean-up efforts. Many students from the entire campus aided in community-wide clean-up efforts. Trees that had been at Davidson for hundreds of years had been uprooted and snapped like match-sticks.

Davidson College canceled classes for this Friday, and no one remembers ever having classes canceled in the college's history! Since there was no electricity, many of the students left and went either to their homes or to friends' homes. That Friday night, several of the InterVarsity students had a prayer and praise service on the steps of Chambers Hall, the large building in the center of campus. Singing praise to God with only candlelight is a memory I will cherish forever. The campus was pitch black; the stars, radiant. It was like being in a ghost town – yet surrounded by brothers and sisters in Christ, praising the Lord by candlelight and flashlights. After the praise service, walking back to Richardson Dorm seemed like a very long walk.

Concerning Hugo, I wrote in my journal:

This weekend God has truly revealed His power to me. As the Hurricane [Hugo] approached and hit the campus, it paralleled the turmoil that I have been feeling inside and it showed the people of Davidson that God controls everything. . . I felt as if God is pushing me to a deeper level of commitment and a more active testimony for Him, and I have been only halfway submitting to and serving Him. This hurricane exemplified God's power and put a lot of things in perspective for me. . .Trees are uprooted that have been here forever, and to God it is just like a puff of breath. 9-24-89

Over and over, God was transforming me through these college years. How was I to know that this transformation was only beginning?

4

God's Vision

As I transitioned from high school to Davidson, I hoped that I could make a fresh start. I still, struggled, however, with past memories of hurt, rejection and insecurity. I realised that changing my environment and acquaintances would not change who I was.

During college my concerns were not about my health but rather about my self-worth. Other people's opinions still bothered me. Did people like me? Would guys ask me out? Could I make the right grades? I wanted to make good grades, choose the right career path, and meet the perfect mate. I often became distracted and discouraged because my eyes would so easily move away from Christ and toward others. Without realizing it, I compared myself to other people. At Davidson, one of the most valuable truths that I discovered was that I am of immeasurable worth in God's sight. His Word assured me that I am valuable in Christ, not because of any worldly attainments I have gained, but because of His grace. The Lord does not make mistakes, and He allows nothing to remain unused.

Growing up, I learned how to win approval

from parents, teachers, youth ministers and thus God (I thought). I knew the right answers and did the right things (sometimes), but I had a shallow understanding of God's grace – His unmerited favor. In some ways I thought I was deserving, although I never would have admitted it. I did not realize that I could do nothing to please Him apart from Christ. So the Lord showed me His mercy and discipline at the same time. I was brought to the lowest point, stripped of all securities, several times, to see that He is ALL. I find that I am still going through these processes, which are part of His making me more like Christ: 'Not that I have already obtained all this, or have already been made perfect, but I press on to take hold of that for which Christ Jesus took hold of me' as the apostle Paul states (Phil. 3:12).

The advertising world tells us that we must be physically fit, driving the fastest car, wearing the right clothes. Evolutionists argue that we evolved from one cell. Many are left wondering 'Who am I?' and 'Why am I here?' More than that, it seems that people with straight hair want curly hair and vice versa. We are not happy with who or where we are.

When I finished college and later worked with college students with RUF (the PCA campus ministry), I would ask the female students about their biggest struggles. Many of them shared with me that they did not like themselves. They wished they had a different body, a more intelligent brain, a keener sense of humor, and the list goes on. I would often direct them to Psalm 139 where we learn that God knows us intimately. He knit us together before we were born, knows our thoughts, numbers our days. He creates each person individually and uniquely, with great care and skill. I believe that we sin by complaining to God about the way He chose to make us. The clay is not supposed to tell the potter what he should do. 'Shall what is formed say to him who formed it, "Why did you make me like this?"' (Rom. 9:20). I would tell these students that you cannot change the fact that you have a big nose or red hair, but you can choose to accept yourself as created in the image of God. As a believer in Christ, God views me in the following ways:[2]

I have peace with God (Romans 5:1)
No longer am I an enemy of God, deserving His holy wrath and justice. Before I received Christ as my Savior, I was at war with God. Everything I did was sinful in His sight. Now I stand before Him in faith. Once redeemed, I have peace with Him.

I am accepted by God (Ephesians 1)
He chose me before the foundation of the world to be His. I am accepted only because of Christ's

righteousness on my behalf. In Him I have redemption according to His grace.

I am a child of God (John 1:12)
As a child, I have access to Him through Jesus. I am an heir and co-heir with Christ.

I am indwelt by the Holy Spirit (1 Corinthians 3:16)
The Spirit lives in me, convicting me of sin and reminding me of God's promises. I am marked with the seal of the Holy Spirit, guaranteeing my inheritance that is to come.

I have access to God's wisdom (James 1:5)
When I need wisdom, God promises to grant me His wisdom. He is all wise and does not withhold anything good from me.

I am helped by God (Hebrews 4:16)
In times of temptation or struggles, He will aid me. He has been my help in the past and is my hope for the years to come. Jesus is my High Priest, able to sympathize with me in my trouble. He is my refuge and shelter in such times.

I am reconciled to God (Romans 5:1)
I am no longer lost but restored to fellowship with God. God's righteous, just anger toward me is removed. I am saved from His wrath.

I have no condemnation (Romans 8:1)
My sin no longer condemns me because Christ paid its penalty. In Christ I am pure because I have His purity. And now I have freedom. I am no longer a prisoner.

I am justified (Romans 5:1)
Legally I have been acquitted, declared innocent. Christ was punished for what I did. The ransom has been paid in full. My debt was paid by Christ.

I have His righteousness (Romans 5:19, 2 Corinthians 5:21)
God sees me robed in Christ's righteousness. In exchange for my sin, He gave me His righteousness. Jesus took the punishment I deserved and gave me the glory rightly His.

I am His representative (2 Corinthians 5:20)
I am an ambassador to declare His goodness and grace. I am called to be a herald, an evangelist, bringing salt and light to the world. Everywhere I go, I bear the mark of Christ.

I am completely forgiven (Colossians 1:14)
My sins past, present and future are removed from me. I no longer have to dwell in my past sin. Because of Christ, there is no need to think about my past sin or to continue wallowing in guilt and self-pity.

I have my needs met by God (Philippians 4:19)
He promises to provide for my every need. He gives me my daily bread, my sustenance for life. I lack nothing. He clothes even the lilies of the field; yes, He will care for me.

I am tenderly loved (Jeremiah 31:3)
God has loved me with an undying love. His love is everlasting, unconditional, undeserving, unshakable, immovable.

I am the aroma of Christ to God (2 Corinthians 2:15)
He takes delight in me. As a living sacrifice, my life is pleasant in God's presence because of Christ. My life is an aroma to those in Christ and to those perishing.

I am a temple of God (1 Corinthians 3:16)
I am now the dwelling place of God. He abides in me and I in Him. His Word is alive and active in me as I hide it in my heart.

I am blameless and beyond reproach (Colossians 1:22)
I have a clean slate before the Lord. My sin has been removed as far as the east is from the west, cast into the bottom of the ocean to be remembered no more.

When we begin to let our emotions dictate our view of ourselves, we must run back to Scripture and renew our minds: 'Do not conform any longer to the pattern of this world, but be transformed by the renewing of your mind' (Rom. 12:2). If the world tells us that we are fat, unattractive rejects, we must remember to have God's vision. His vision is clear and true.

Journal entry from 8-13-90

> In the blackness of the night
> In the silence of the night
> In the depth of my heart
> Lord, You can reach.
> Grace, grace, God's grace –
> Grace that is greater than all my sin!

God demonstrated His love for me first by sacrificing His Son on my behalf. He later showed me His love by saving me from physical death during open-heart surgery.

5

R U Flexible?

As a college senior, if asked, I would not have initially described myself as flexible. Actually, I was very driven, having a Type A personality (a personality characterised as one that is self-motivated and goal-orientated). I was learning to be more adaptable, especially after spending the previous summer on a mattress in an unfurnished room and working with inner-city kids in Nashville, Tennessee.

Having grown up in the South and seeing prejudice and racism, I wanted to make a difference in the lives of inner-city children. Davidson's InterVarsity had taken groups to Awareness Weekend in Charlotte, North Carolina, to work in soup kitchens, build houses with Habitat for Humanity and to paint Christ the King Center, a ministry in downtown Charlotte. I enjoyed these weekends and felt a burden for the inner-city. I did not really know how I could minister in the inner-city, but I wanted to be available.

An opportunity arose for the summer of 1990, between my junior and senior year in college, to spend it as an intern for Mercy Ministries of the

Presbyterian Church in America in the Edgehill Housing Community, an inner-city low income housing project in Nashville I had never even been to Nashville! I would be working with a program called Summer of Champions, an academic and spiritual enrichment program for elementary students in the Edgehill community. I needed to raise $800 to cover my room and board for eight weeks. As the summer drew closer, I received a call from Mr. Stan Weber, the leader of this ministry, who informed me that another young lady, Stefanie Kimmerlin (now Ellison) would be joining me. Stan said that Stefanie and I would be living in the Webers' attic in the inner-city neighborhood. However, a few days before our arrival date, Stan called again and told me about a fire that had burned only their attic. There would be a change of plans: Stefanie and I would stay with the female ministry staff person who lived in a townhouse (not in the inner-city neighborhood). My mother was a bit relieved!

Of the $800 to be raised, I received a partial grant from Davidson College which was awarded to students who were volunteering their summer vacation for service. I spent the night before my departure for Nashville with my aunt in Birmingham, Alabama. After I loaded the car, they followed me to the interstate. I looked in the rearview mirror and waved good-bye. My thought was, 'Here I go.' I felt scared, alone, and unsure, but excited because I knew that God was calling me there. I left without even having the whole $800. I did not want to raise support or to ask my parents for money although they would have freely given what I needed. To be honest, my mother was not too thrilled with the inner city ministry idea because she worried that something might happen to me. I knew that if God wanted me in Nashville for the summer, He would protect me and shield me from danger. Trusting that God would provide for the remainder of my expenses, off I went.

I arrived in Nashville, found the place where I would be staying and met Stefanie and Carey, the owner of this wonderful townhouse. Our room was the only unfurnished one – Stefanie and I managed with two mattresses and one lamp which sat on a milk crate. We did not see Carey very often once the Summer of Champions began because Carey worked in the ministry office and was busy at night. Since Carey had grown up in Nashville, she had family and friends with whom she spent time regularly. Stefanie and I ventured around Nashville, getting to know each other, exploring the Davis-Kidd Bookstore and Food Lion, and window shopping at the Green Hills Mall.

During the first few days in Nashville, Stefanie and I met Stan Weber and his family, toured the ministry office and jumped into helping with VBS at Christ Presbyterian Church. We became familiar with the church property and met some of the individuals who would also be volunteering with the Summer of Champions, our inner-city program. While working with VBS at Christ Presbyterian Church, I met a lady whose husband owned a telemarketing business and needed several people to work at night. I told her that I was interested in earning some extra money, and she gave me his telephone number. This telemarketing job involved calling individuals and asking them about health care services in their area. Since I like talking on the phone, I enjoyed asking people about treatment they had received at their local hospital. After a few nights of phone calls, I had earned the remainder of the money that I needed for the summer.

Also, two of my InterVarsity friends from Davidson were living in Nashville that summer: Bill Wilson and Robert Austell. Bill was volunteering with a record company during the day and working some nights at O'Charleys Restaurant. Robert was volunteering with an advertising company. When I found out about this night job, I let both of them know; and they were able to earn a few extra dollars too.

Stefanie and I spent the second week going door to door in the projects and telling the kids about the summer program. Finally, the actual Summer of Champions began! It was set up so that the Christ Presbyterian bus would pick up children in the mornings and take them to Christ Presbyterian Church. Each day would begin with a chapel service. Then children would go to their respective classrooms and spend time on mathematics, reading, science and other activities. They had a break for lunch, which was provided, and an afternoon of PE and arts and crafts.

Part of the summer program consisted of going to an overnight camp, the Smoky Mountain Church Camp, for a week. Most of the children had never stayed in a cabin in the woods – and they were ecstatic! It was a true adventure for me too! I laughed a lot at their reactions to insects and 'outdoor' sounds. They made interesting crafts, climbed a ropes course, and many learned to swim for the first time. It gave me great joy to watch the children learn their memory verses (from Ephesians 6:10-17) while at this overnight camp. Knowing that they memorized these verses gives me hope that these children are still standing strong for Christ wherever they may be.

While that summer was an awesome experience, I struggled a great deal as well. I doubted my effectiveness with these particular kids and in ministry in general. The Lord continued to show me my sin and pride as He began slowly chiseling away these unrighteous aspects of my life. One of the younger children, about seven years old, whose name was Ramona, was a difficult child who did not respect adults. Ramona always talked back, used curse words and hit others. One day while we were at the Smoky Mountain Church Camp, I went for a walk down the mountain in order to enjoy a reflective prayer time. I was frustrated with Ramona. I remember praying about Ramona, her attitude and behavior.

Then I realized, 'I am Ramona.' I saw that my heart was just as dark and selfish as Ramona's, apart from God's marvelous grace. At that time, I remembered an old saying my father taught me: 'But for the grace of God, there go I.' Vividly and shockingly, I saw that I was, as a sinner, in exactly the same standing as Ramona – deserving God's wrath. For some unknown reason, however, God chose me to be His child. Not only did God adopt me as His, but He blessed me with every spiritual and material blessing because of His goodness. I had become the Pharisee whom Jesus describes in Luke 18:10-11: 'Two men went up to the temple to pray, one a Pharisee and the other a tax collector. The Pharisee stood up and prayed about himself: "God, I thank you that I am not like other men – robbers, evildoers, adulterers – or even like this tax collector.'" I was horrified at the sinfulness in my heart. The Lord reminded me that Ramona, one of eight or nine children living with her elderly grandmother, had not known her biological mother and father for one reason or another. It was as if He said, 'I have been gracious to you, an undeserving sinner. Can you not show grace to Ramona, who does not even have half the material blessings I have given you?'

Inevitably, I developed a new love for Ramona after this realisation. Since the Summer of Champions, I have often wondered where Ramona is and what may have happened to her. Ramona gave me insight into my own sinfulness, and this moment of self-awareness will remain etched in my memory forever.

Returning from my summer in Nashville, I began my senior year at Davidson and did not know exactly what to do with a major in British and American Literature. I applied for teaching positions in several different settings: teaching English in Japan, teaching in the inner-city and teaching in a private secondary school setting. I even considered a career in journalism. My maternal grandfather had been a journalist, and I had sensed subtle pressures to continue in his footsteps. While I enjoyed interviewing people, gathering facts and obtaining the latest news, my heart's desire was to be involved in full-time Christian ministry.

In February 1991, I literally stumbled upon Reformed University Fellowship (RUF), the campus ministry of the Presbyterian Church in America (PCA). Since I was already a member of the PCA denomination, I was drawn to this campus ministry. I wanted to know more about it. While I had heard the name, RUF, I was completely unfamiliar with its purpose, goals, prevalence and philosophy. There was not an RUF group at Davidson. At that time, there were no RUFs in North Carolina. Throughout that weekend in February, I regularly met individuals who had grown in Christ through the ministry of RUF.

As we loaded up one van and several cars, about twenty students from the Davidson InterVarsity group drove to Orlando, Florida, that February for the annual Ligonier Conference with featured speakers such as R. C. Sproul, Joni Eareckson-Tada and Steve Brown. We began our trek on Friday afternoon, around 1 p.m. and arrived in Orlando later that night. Therefore, we missed all of the speakers on the first night. We were staying with two Davidson alumni who were attending Reformed Theological Seminary (RTS) in Orlando and with a family whose children had attended Davidson. Thankfully, we each paid the student rate for the conference with the understanding that we would attend a dinner for prospective RTS students.

During the weekend, I kept meeting people who had been involved with RUF groups on their college campuses. First I met Bill Tennyson, a guy who had worked with my friend Robert Austell in Nashville the previous summer. Bill asked about my post-graduation plans. As I mentioned several of my ideas, I stressed that I was also considering full-time ministry. I explained that I did not think God was leading me to InterVarsity staff, mainly because I did not want to make a four-year commitment to anything at that point. Furthermore, I discussed with Bill the difficulties of inviting guest speakers to Davidson's InterVarsity large group each week. There seemed to be a lack of consistency in varying weekly messages. In addition, I told him that I was uncomfortable and uncertain about discipling male students and speaking at large group meetings.

At this time Bill shared with me that he had become a Christian through RUF at Mississippi State University, and he began to describe RUF to me. In 1991 there were thirty-six RUF groups on campuses in the United States, each one with an ordained PCA pastor or seminary student and some with interns. RUF has a two-fold purpose: reaching students for Christ and equipping them to serve. I enjoyed hearing that RUF is set up as an arm of the church, not as a parachurch organization. Campus ministers view their ministry as a continuation of nurturing covenant children. So when they hear of PCA students coming to their campuses, they try to meet them and introduce them to RUF. Each of the campus ministers has a high regard for the church. They encourage students to attend church and not to consider their weekly RUF meeting as a substitute for church.

There are four presuppositions of RUF: growth in grace, fellowship and service, evangelism and missions, and Biblical world and life view. As I was listening to Bill describe various aspects of RUF, I found that I was agreeing at every point. Furthermore, the intern program was established as a two-year learning/ministry position. And the female interns only teach and disciple other female students. Everything that Bill described sounded great, but the applications had been due about six months earlier.

During the weekend, Bill introduced me to Todd Teller, who was then an RUF intern at Mississippi State. Todd subsequently gave me more information about who to contact concerning the intern program. Making RUF sound like an effective campus ministry, Todd arranged for me to meet another person who had been impacted through this work. In God's sovereignty, as a college senior seeking His will, I had met three people who introduced me to this new campus ministry.

As soon as I returned from Orlando, I called the RUM (nationally referred to as Reformed University Ministries while locally called Reformed University Fellowship) office in Atlanta and asked for an application. Later I visited the RUF ministry at Clemson University and met the female staff person, Jerdone Davis. During my spring break, I proceeded with the intern selection procedure and met with the South Carolina campus ministry committee of the South Carolina presbytery. This committee interviewed me along with two other prospective interns. After much prayer and discussion with my parents, I followed God's leading to become an intern. On that Monday in May, the day after my graduation from Davidson College in 1991, I went to Panama City Beach, Florida to start my first day as an RUF intern. During this week I met the other beginning interns, and we began staff-training together while RUF held its annual summer conference for students.

I discovered the day before graduation that my campus assignment would be The University of Alabama, although it was written nowhere on my campus preference list. My top two choices were Vanderbilt and Clemson – not Alabama! I had a misinformed view of Alabama and initially was not excited at all. In my mind, all of the 'wild' students went to Alabama. Thankfully, while I was at the RUF Summer Conference, I met Billy Joseph who was the RUF campus minister at Alabama. We discovered that we were both from Trinity Church in Montgomery, and we began to establish a good working relationship. He introduced me to students from Alabama who were attending the Summer Conference and provided tips for me about when and where to look for housing in Tuscaloosa. Even though I was upset about my assignment to Alabama at first, it ended up being a wonderful location. Not only was it close to home, but it was also close to UAB Hospital.

Before classes started, I went to Tuscaloosa and found a studio apartment to rent. My apartment was a duplex, owned by the man who lived next door in a house. It was one big room with a tiny bathroom and tiny kitchen, but just right for me! My first semester was spent trying to meet students and get my bearings. Since I did not have a television, I spent time reading, painting and listening to the radio. I also enjoyed inviting groups of RUF students over for games and fellowship. Occasionally, I went running in my neighborhood, where I acquired the nickname 'Tasty Legs.' While I was jogging one afternoon, I was attacked by a neighbor's Chow dog. So, life in Tuscaloosa was not without some difficulty.

During the second semester, I taught Bible studies and became more involved in students' lives. I was also learning a lot from the RUF intern study program in which all interns participated. Examining the New Testament, reading *The Westminster Confession of Faith*, and memorising the first forty questions of *The Shorter Catechism* were our assignments during the first year. The following summer (1992), the RUF interns had staff training in Jackson, Mississippi, for one week in June and later for two weeks in July.

Before I went for staff training in July, I was due for a cardiology check up. However, since my last visit with Dr. Bargeron, he had retired. My parents knew of a new female cardiologist in Montgomery, Dr. Wynne Crawford, who had begun attending their church. I liked the idea of going to a female cardiologist, and so I scheduled an appointment to see her. The heart echo test, done during my visit with Dr. Crawford, showed that I needed to have an aortic valve replacement. Dr. Crawford explained that the aortic valve insufficiency was causing my heart to become enlarged. She referred me to Dr. James Kirklin at UAB since he was the primary aortic valve specialist in Alabama. At that time, Dr. Crawford also knew that UAB Hospital had the latest technology for open-heart surgery.

I remember telling my parents what Dr. Crawford had told me, and they were in a state of disbelief. They decided to meet with Dr. Crawford for a consultation while I was away at staff training in Jackson. She explained that surgery was not urgent but that I would need it within the next year. All of us scheduled an appointment to see Dr. Kirklin in Birmingham and discovered that he would be the surgeon. While Dr. Kirklin told us that many individuals each year have aortic valve replacements, he noted that complications are not too frequent. Mom, Dad and I all believed that this would be a 'routine' surgery.

As a joke, RUF stands for 'Are You Flexible?' It seems that interns and campus ministers would always tell stories about adapting to different, peculiar, unexpected situations within the ministry. I am so thankful that I found flexibility to be true within this ministry. When they heard that I needed surgery, all of the RUF administrators and campus ministers were adaptable; their main concern, my well-being. I scheduled the surgery for the beginning of the fall semester, 1992, not anticipating any complications and hoping to be back on campus within a few weeks. I never received one disgruntled remark from the RUF staff, only encouragement.

During the entire hospital stay, I received continual prayers and visits, not only from RUF administrators and campus ministers, but cards from every RUF group in the country and from many students. I am thankful to have been surrounded by brothers and sisters in the Lord during this time – many of whom I did not know personally were praying for me.

6

Standing on Solid Ground

Many individuals have asked, along with Rabbi Harold Kushner, why does God allow bad things to happen to good people? Kushner's answer is that God is perplexed when bad things happen. Kushner believes that things happen by chance. My response to Kushner is, first of all, there are no 'good people!' We have all sinned, but thankfully Christians are saved by grace. Secondly, God allows suffering to occur in our lives so that He may be glorified.

How can He be glorified through our trials?

God is glorified as His children endure trials with grace. Suffering occurs in many forms, as J. C. Ryle describes in his book, *Holiness*: 'If you are a believer, you must reckon on having your share of sickness and pain, of sorrow and tears, of losses and crosses, of deaths and bereavements, of partings and separations, of vexations and disappointments, as long as you are in the body.'[3] During the life of the Apostle Paul, Christians were persecuted, beaten, imprisoned and banished. Yet they did not lose hope. Second Corinthians 4:8-9 describes one of the 'paradoxes' of the Christian faith: 'We are hard pressed on every side, but not crushed; perplexed, but not in despair; persecuted, but not abandoned; struck down, but not destroyed.' Suffering goes hand in hand with being a Christian.

How can Christians face such difficulties and yet live? As D. Martyn Lloyd-Jones explains in his book *Spiritual Depression*: 'Very well, these things may be found at one and the same time, and the Christian must never regard himself as one who is exempt from natural feelings. He has something that enables him to rise above these things, but the glory of the Christian life is that you rise above them though you feel them. It is not an absence of feeling.'[4] We experience real feelings of hurt, despair, loneliness and abandonment. However, we are to, as J. I. Packer writes in *Knowing God*, 'Think against your feelings; argue yourself out of the gloom they have spread; unmask the unbelief they have nourished . . . look up from your problems to the God of the gospel; let evangelical thinking correct emotional thinking.'[5] We must think of our lives as the tapestry, only seeing the back side, the broken, knotted threads, mixed and mingled, appearing to be a hodgepodge. Our mind must reassure us that we will not see the beautifully finished work until we are with Christ. Only then will the back make sense. We will one day see the purposes of our trials, woven together creatively.

God is glorified as He chastises us, removing sin from our lives. As Hebrews 12:6, 7 describes: 'Because the Lord disciplines those he loves, and he punishes everyone he accepts as a son. Endure hardship as discipline; God is treating you as sons.' The Father will chastise His children – for their good – sometimes to wake them from slackness. Often we are courting sins in our lives, not willing to put them to death. Our Lord is jealous, not wanting our hearts to belong to anything but Himself. He sometimes allows us to suffer to prune those petty sins from our lives.

Another reason God allows us to endure this 'heaviness' is to prepare us for something else. Remember the life of Joseph, sold into slavery by his brothers. Later he was set up and accused of trying to sleep with his master Potiphar's wife. After being rejected by his brothers and unjustly imprisoned, Joseph must have wondered what the Lord was doing. Eventually, Joseph was called upon by Pharaoh to interpret his dreams. Rather than seizing personal glory for his accurate interpretations, Joseph announced to Pharaoh: 'I cannot do it, but God will give Pharaoh the answer he desires' (Gen. 41:16). All of Joseph's trials were preparing him for upcoming days during which he would be in charge of Pharaoh's entire kingdom. Finally, Joseph was able to reunite with his father and brothers and rescue them from the famine in their land. As Joseph greeted his brothers, he encouraged them with truth: 'Am I in the place of God? You intended to harm me, but God intended it for good to accomplish what is now being done, the saving of many lives' (Gen. 50:19-20). The Scripture contains numerous other examples of saints who endured hardships as preparation for something greater.

We have hope that all things work together for good, as Paul reminds believers in Romans 8. Furthermore, we know that: 'If God is for us, who can be against us?' (Rom. 8:31). As Packer encourages in *Knowing God*: 'Or if you are a true believer, and He still puts thorns in your bed, it is only to keep you from falling into the somnolence of complacency, and for the need to bring you back constantly in self-abasement and faith to seek His face.... It is a discipline of love, and must be received accordingly.'[6] Even though trials do not seem loving at the time, we must trust in the innate goodness of God.

Job's life exemplifies how we must face trials. Satan had returned from roaming around the earth when God asked him if he had considered Job, an upright, blameless man. Then God gave Satan permission to test Job without taking his life. God still had ultimate control. Job's faith was tested as he lost everything, even his friends and health. Yet he did not curse God. 'The LORD gave and the LORD has taken away; may the name of the LORD be praised' (Job 1:21). Job placed his hope in God, 'Though he slay me, yet will I hope in him.' And Job understood that his faith would be made stronger as a result of the trials: 'When he has tested me, I shall come forth as gold' (Job 13:15; 23:10). After Job survived numerous losses and difficulties, the Lord restored him to health and prosperity.

Our Father also allows his children to endure hardships as a means of faith development. As Peter describes: 'These [trials] have come so that your faith – of greater worth than gold, which perishes even though refined by fire – may be proved genuine and may result in praise, glory and honor when Jesus Christ is revealed' (1 Peter 1:7). It is certainly easier to trust God when our lives are unfolding smoothly. However, when difficulties arise, which they will, our faith is strengthened. 'We can say: "Yes, I know, I do not see the sun but I know it is there. I know that behind the clouds the Face of God is looking upon me." It is by means of these trials that that element of trust is developed.'[7] When we encounter trials, our true faith is proven. 'Trouble is often the fire which will burn away the dross that clings to our hearts. Trouble is the only pruning knife which the great Husbandman employs in order to make us fruitful in good works.'[8] Just as the metals must be refined in fire, so our faith is shown genuine through trials.

Trials plague believers in order to remind us that we are nothing and Christ is everything. We are needy, helpless children. Yet, He promises not to give us more than we can bear: 'No temptation has seized you except what is common to man. And God is faithful; he will not let you be tempted beyond what you can bear' (1 Cor. 10:13). Too often, we look at our grey clouds rather than the Maker of the clouds. We cannot see beyond this moment of anguish, much less imagine anything positive or useful resulting from our heartache. However, we are promised that our faith, that is being strengthened and tested, will be found praiseworthy at the Lord's return. Because of His covenant commitment to us, God will keep His promises. He is the Rock on which we must stand when the world seems to fall around us.

Since I was unconscious during the surgery and serious complications, I asked several friends what they learned as they reflected on my critical condition. One theme resounding in their answers has been that believers must be standing on solid ground. Jesus says in Matthew 7:24: 'Therefore everyone who hears these words of mine and puts them into practice is like a wise man who built his house on the rock. The rain came down, the streams rose, and the winds blew and beat against that house; yet it did not fall, because it had its foundation on the rock.'

John Hunter, one of the students on the leadership team of our RUF group at Alabama, heard the news while at the beach for the beginning-of-the semester student leadership team retreat. One person received a telephone call from the hospital, entered the room, and told the group that the doctors were trying hard to keep me alive because of reactions and complications. Confused and frustrated, John was 'shaken up' and said that it was difficult for the group to understand the report's seriousness in the 'light, fun' atmosphere. Also, because these students were hours away and did not have specific details about the complications, they relied on Christ alone for my protection. According to John, due to the situation's endlessness and complexity, total dependence upon God became a reality for him.

A few days later, John came to the hospital and described the mood around the hospital as peaceful. A group of people went to the chapel to pray that God would do His pleasure. 'They prayed not that God would spare you,' said John, 'but that God would do His pleasure. It was a letting go and selfless prayer. The miracle is not that you're alive,' added John, 'but that any of us are alive and that God allows us to live.'

According to John, 'Several individuals evaluated their real positions before God – that they had no right to question.' Nothing but Christ proved to be solid; thus, worthy concerns sharply contrasted with and weeded away extravagant matters. 'It was truly an act of grace that God allowed you to come out okay,' said John.

Alabama's RUF campus minister, Billy Joseph, described his feelings during this time: 'For me, it was a time to see God's sovereignty in action. From my own perspective, I was faced with my own inadequacy. It was overwhelming. The reality was that I could do nothing but listen and be available. I remember standing in the recovery room with Margaret's Mom and Dad, looking at her with all the attachments to keep her alive. There was nothing I could say; there was nothing I could do. All I could do was trust that God was in charge. Later we went to the UAB chapel to pray and read Scripture. My mind went blank as to what to read. I stumbled through Psalms, reading one after another simply to hear what God said about anything. I tried to encourage Mr. and Mrs. Carroll and William, but nothing seemed to fit. What was I doing there trying to help them? I had nothing to offer but God's Word.'

My mother and father exemplified what it

means to stand on solid ground. During the night of the surgery, the doctors were not sure if I would live or die. My parents stayed in the small waiting room outside the CICU (Cardiac Intensive Care Unit). Finally, one of the nurses brought them several pillows. My mother remembered the doctors telling her that I was in bad shape. She and my dad spent the entire night in the tiny room, singing hymns, the doxology, and praise songs together. Although they were completely helpless to save me, they relied on the Rock. As the nurse came in and asked if they would like to see me, my mother asked him if she could touch me. 'I did not know if they would let me touch you,' she later told me. Thus, they stood over their only girl, watching her struggle for life. Still they did not lose hope in God.

Billy Joseph remembers my parents' witness to others: 'Another interesting thing was the opportunity for the Carroll family to minister to another family that was also going through a rough time with their son. I can't remember the details, but the Carrolls were always ready to speak words of comfort to this other family at the same time they were going through difficult times themselves. It was neat to see God use them in this other family's life.'

During my illness and long recovery, I often wondered if God was punishing me for some unconfessed sin in my heart. I was reminded of John 9:1-3 in which the disciples and Jesus encounter a man who was born blind:

'As he went along, he saw a man blind from birth. His disciples asked him, "Rabbi, who sinned, this man or his parents, that he was born blind?" "Neither this man nor his parents sinned," said Jesus, "but this happened so that the work of God might be displayed in his life. . . . I am the light of the world."' Like the blind man, I was born with a misformed aortic valve. After much soul-searching, I finally concluded that this birth defect existed so that God would somehow reveal His glory in me.

About a month before my surgery I wrote:

Making in me a quiet place,
Time and effort, lots of space,
Stripped of all worldly gain,
I carry my cross, bearing the pain.
My Savior calls, I must go
Whichever way He will show.
Nothing I have but Him alone,
Longing for an eternal home.   (7-15-92)

I could not have conceived what was about to happen to me as I faced the operating table. Before this surgery, I would have intellectually agreed with the Bible's promises about suffering and becoming more like Christ. In 1992 I had to put my intellect into practice as I underwent trauma of dramatic proportions. Scripture encourages us to 'endure hardship as discipline; ... No discipline seems pleasant at the time, but painful. Later on, however, it produces a harvest of righteousness and peace for those who have been trained by it' (Heb. 12:7, 11). The discipline is not enjoyable, but it glorifies Christ in ways incomprehensible to us.

Both Christians and non-Christians face hardships. Billy Joseph once told me that he believes that when an unbeliever is stricken with cancer, a believer will be diagnosed with cancer also so that the world may see how Christians handle adversity. Billy's idea is not really Biblically based, but it makes sense. Christians are to be 'other worldly', which is one of the things God has shown me through my surgery. Second Corinthians is one of my favorite books because it points so clearly to our true home: 'But we have this treasure in jars of clay to show that this all-surpassing power is from God and not from us ... Therefore we do not lose heart. Though outwardly we are wasting away, yet inwardly we are being renewed day by day. For our light and momentary troubles are achieving for us an eternal glory that far outweighs them all. So we fix our eyes not on what is seen, but on what is unseen. For what is seen is temporary, but what is unseen is eternal' (2 Cor. 4:7, 16-18). Even though we may not understand why God allows Christians or non-Christians to suffer, nor can we see the good in these hardships, we must continue standing on solid ground.

A few days before the surgery I wrote in my journal:

There is only one doctor in Alabama who does this procedure, and he is at UAB. When I think of what a heart looks like and how a valve works, I am afraid and concerned and just ignorant of how it would look when the doctor cuts me open. I turn my thoughts to my God who created my heart, and my fears are gone. He withholds knowledge from me as a blessing. I believe I'd be overwhelmed if I could see all that would happen. (7-25-92)

'My hope is built on nothing less
than Jesus' blood and righteousness;
I dare not trust the sweetest frame
But wholly lean on Jesus' name.

On Christ the solid rock I stand;
All other ground is sinking sand,
All other ground is sinking sand!'

(Edward Mote)

7

August 21 1992

This day is hard for me to describe because I was unconscious. I was admitted to UAB Hospital on Thursday, August 20th, at 11 a.m. and had an echo-cardiogram as soon as I arrived. This heart echo test analyzes the sequences of blood-flow through the heart, thus measuring how well the heart functions. After noon on Thursday, I was not allowed to eat or drink anything. Several RUF staff members and other friends came by to visit me that day. Later Thursday night I remember nurses coming to shave my entire body – how humiliating! The following morning, Friday, August 21st, 1992, very early, the nurses came in to administer anaesthesia and to take me to the operating room. My mother started crying and said, 'We'll see you real soon.' I remember telling her to stop crying because she did not sound too convincing. From that point until weeks later, I had no idea what was happening.

Most heart valve replacement surgeries last approximately two to four hours. Doctors make an incision through the breast bone and then stop the heart. Blood continues to circulate through the bypass (or heart lung) machine. Once the doctors examine the valve, they may determine that it can be repaired. If not, they replace it with one of three types: pig, mechanical, or human valve. After suturing the new valve into position, doctors disconnect the patient from the bypass machine and sew up the incision. Usually, patients remain in the Intensive Care Unit for twenty-four hours and are discharged within a few days. It seems a fairly 'routine' procedure.

During my consultation with Dr. Kirklin before the surgery, I requested a human valve rather than a mechanical or pig valve. In most cases, the human valve (homograft) lasts longer (twelve to fifteen years) than the others and does not require on-going medication. Individuals with this type of implanted valve are also able to have children. Dr. Kirklin assured me that he would try to use a human valve. If, for some reason, he could not use a homograft, Dr. Kirklin would use a mechanical valve, which also lasts between twelve and fifteen years but requires that the recipient take blood thinner. The pig valve, my third choice, only lasts five to seven years. Therefore, I believed that a human valve would last the longest and would be most similar to my own valve.

Around six or seven hours after the operation began, my parents finally received a phone call from one of the doctors who said that the main part of the surgery was finished: however, that they were having a hard time getting me off the bypass machine. According to Dr. Crawford, who was continually updated by Dr. Kirkin: 'As the doctors finished the surgery and started to close, they noted a drop in blood pressure and a marked rise in heart rate. Your abdomen began to swell alarmingly, and they realised that you had suddenly accumulated a large amount of fluid in your abdomen. A catheter was placed in the abdomen, releasing a large amount of fluid, about two liters, I think. At that time he (Dr. Kirkin) called it a rare anaphylactic reaction to a bypass.' My body had experienced an allergic or chemical reaction to the bypass machine, an unpredictable incident which occurs approximately once in 50,000 times. Dr. Robert Bourge, my present cardiologist, immediately reviewed my case and began assisting Dr. Kirklin at this time. Recently he told me that the type of reaction I had remains unknown. However, it was not caused by latex gloves or cleaning fluids or other disposable components. A few hours later, a doctor called again and asked my parents for permission to use an artificial heart to help my heart continue beating.

This artificial heart consisted of a left ventricular assist device (LVAD) and a right ventricular assist device (RVAD), with a respirator. They also connected me to a machine nicknamed 'the Cell Saver' because it recovers blood lost during and after surgery, filters it and gives it back to the patient (preventing additional transfusions). At that time, the assist machines were experimental. Now, however, because of medical advancements, individuals waiting for heart transplants sometimes live by these machines for sixteen to eighteen months. These Assist machines are placed on the left side of the body, near the diaphragm, connecting to the heart with two tubes to provide pumping for the heart. An external air vent leads out of the body. My heart was not functioning at all on its own – only through these machines. My parents did not know what to expect.

At around 11 p.m., one doctor told my parents that things were not going well. They decided to place me on an emergency heart transplant list. At that time, I returned from the operating room and my parents went into the CICU to see me, along with Billy Joseph (campus minister of RUF at Alabama) and Joseph Wheat, pastor of Trinity Presbyterian Church in Tuscaloosa. My parents described me as being swollen like the blueberry in Willy Wonka and surrounded by machines on every side with about three nurses monitoring them. I began to respond to voices by squeezing their hands. The doctors decided that I was stable although very critical. Even Dr. Bourge admitted that he informed my family of my condition and prognosis. 'I was very worried that you would not survive the ordeal,' he said. After the first night, everyone had to wait and see what would happen.

8

Pray Without Ceasing

Prayer is one of the reasons I am alive today. God commands all believers to pray without ceasing: 'Be joyful always; pray continually; give thanks in all circumstances, for this is God's will for you in Christ Jesus' (1 Thess. 5:16-18). Christians are instructed to pray always, not just in a crisis. Yet so many of us do not pray unless we are in need. Our prayers are to have several components, not just lists of people who are sick. Through prayer, we are to praise God, confess our sins, thank Him for everything, and lastly make personal requests.

When I was in need, people all over the United States and the world prayed for me. Many still pray about my health today. Prayer encourages fellow believers, and God delights in our prayers, according to Proverbs 15:8: '. . . but the prayer of the upright pleases him.'

Continual prayer does not necessarily mean a literal, uninterrupted prayer. If this were so, we would not have time to work and participate in our daily activities. Prayer without ceasing, however, refers to our lifestyle. We are to continually live an exposed life, our hearts directed toward God. This prayer without ceasing is a lifestyle posture. Our communication with God is to be constantly open. When we sin, we are to confess it so that our line with God remains unhindered. 'Why is prayer necessary for Christians? Because it is the chief part of the gratitude which God requires of us, and because God will give his grace and Holy Spirit only to those who sincerely beseech him in prayer without ceasing, and who thank him for these gifts' (*The Heidelberg Catechism*, Q116). Colossians challenges, 'Devote yourselves to prayer, being watchful and thankful' (4:2). As we watch, we are able to thank God for His richest blessings.

Many prayed faithfully for my recovery. Trinity Presbyterian Churches in Tuscaloosa and Montgomery, along with Eastwood Presbyterian, and my North Carolina church connections prayed weekly for me. Students at Davidson held a twenty-four hour prayer vigil for me, and the InterVarsity group prayed regularly. Davidson alumni maintained a prayer chain, wherein one person would obtain the update and then phone others. My dear friends, Laurie and Tom Tolbert, Hamilton Williams, Kristi Kessler, Jennifer Brown, Bruce Page and many others, prayed. Furthermore, RUF staff people and students participated in prayer chains on my behalf.

At Covenant Theological Seminary, former

RUF interns, Charles Godwin and Todd Teller would ask their classes to pray for me daily when the professors would ask for prayer requests. When I was able to visit the seminary in March 1993, many people remembered my name and said, 'You are the person we have been praying for.' Each RUF group prayed as they remained updated on my progress. Churches large and small gathered and lifted prayers on my behalf. Todd Teller's mother asked her prayer group in Vicksburg, Mississippi, to pray; and Charles Godwin's grandparents and their church in Meridian, Mississippi, prayed too. On a trip to Mentone, Alabama, during July 1993, my mother and I met a lady who belongs to a church in Mississippi who had been praying for me each week.

In addition, Jackie Walker, a former Alabama RUF student, was in Australia doing a short-term mission trip when she heard the news about my surgery. Joe and Alice Parker, missionaries from my parents' church, were on the team with Jackie. Later, Jackie told me that they prayed all night long when the news from UAB Hospital was very discouraging. Carolyn Phillips, a life-long friend and short-term missionary in Milan, Italy, asked all of the Italian Christians to pray. Relatives in Equador were praying as well, along with their churches.

Billy Joseph recalls: 'The Alabama students prayed regularly for Margaret as well as for her family. Each RUF group meeting was a key time for prayer. Prayer was the main way for the students to minister to Margaret. They also let their friends know to pray as well. For those weeks RUF, Campus Crusade for Christ, FCA and Calvary Baptist Collegiate Ministry there at Alabama had Margaret as their common prayer request. RUFs from all over the denomination also were praying. The RUM intern class Margaret was in let their RUFs know to be in prayer. The local PCA churches were focused on Margaret in their prayers. The churches of the Presbytery of Southeast Alabama and Warrior Presbytery were in prayer for Margaret. Churches all over the south, the U.S. and the world were in prayer for Margaret. It was truly a blessing to see God's people so focused on the need of one of His children.'

Not only did friends, family members and churches pray continually, but they also prayed with peace. When family and friends prayed in the hospital chapel on numerous occasions, my father (as I have been told) always prayed not for God to heal me but rather that He do His will. My father knew that I might not recover or that I might never be able to walk, talk and enjoy things the way that I once had. However, he continued to pray that God be glorified whether I recovered fully or remained comatose or whatever the consequences. Philippians 4:6 encourages believers in this kind of prayer: 'Do not be anxious about anything, but in everything, by prayer and petition, with thanksgiving, present your requests to God. And the peace of God, which transcends all understanding, will guard your hearts and your minds in Christ Jesus.' Through his prayers, my father was a testimony to many, praying with peace, asking for God's will, whether it was for me to live or to die.

These prayers contained power. 'This is the confidence we have in approaching God: that if we ask anything according to his will, he hears us. And if we know that he hears us – whatever we ask – we know that we have what we asked of him' (1 John 5:14-15). And we do not have to be Super Christian to be used in prayer. James tells us, 'Elijah was a man just like us. He prayed earnestly that it would not rain, and it did not rain on the land for three and a half years. Again he prayed, and the heavens gave rain, and the earth produced its crops' (James 5:17-18). God does not promise that if we ask for a new sportscar it will automatically be ours, but He assures us that He hears our cry. If we ask for His will to be done, it is.

Our model for prayer comes from The Lord's

Prayer as Jesus taught His disciples how to pray. *The Westminster Shorter Catechism* describes prayer: 'What is prayer? Prayer is an offering up of our desires unto God for things agreeable to his will, in the name of Christ, with confession of our sins, and thankful acknowledgment of his mercies' (Q98). It is mind-boggling to think that we can speak to the Maker of the Universe – and that He hears us! When we pray, we approach God with child-like dependence and with holy reverence. We beseech Him to provide for our daily necessities, confessing our sins and asking Him to make us able to submit to His will in all things. Paul calls believers to pray in Ephesians 6:18: 'And pray in the Spirit on all occasions with all kinds of prayers and requests. With this in mind, be alert and always keep on praying for all the saints.' We are to be like Epaphras, 'always wrestling in prayer for you' (Col. 4:12). Prayer is not an option for believers; it is our life-line, our support and connection to the Source.

While God chose for me to recover, His answer is not always what we desire. Often we pray with selfish motivations. However, by the time our request reaches His throne of grace, the Spirit has transformed our prayers to be in conformity with His will. I heard this principle of prayer illustrated as a cake-decorating tool. The baker clumps icing into the canvas end of the cake-decorating tool (our prayers); but when the icing passes through the decorating tip, it appears in beautiful patterns and perfect form. 'In the same way, the Spirit helps us in our weakness. We do not know what we ought to pray for, but the Spirit himself intercedes for us with groans that words cannot express. And he who searches our hearts knows the mind of the Spirit, because the Spirit intercedes for the saints in accordance with God's will' (Rom. 8:26-27). Even if the Lord answers our prayer with 'No' or 'Wait,' we must be submissive to His larger plan for our lives, knowing that His will is being accomplished.

As I think back about all of the people who prayed for me even when the situation seemed hopeless, I am reminded of the parable of the persistent widow. This woman continued to ask the judge for justice. As Jesus told the disciples: 'For some time he refused. But finally he said to himself, "Even though I don't fear God or care about men, yet because this widow keeps bothering me, I will see that she gets justice, so that she won't eventually wear me out with her coming!"' Adding commentary, Jesus said, 'And will not God bring about justice for his chosen ones, who cry out to him day and night?' (Luke 18:4-5, 7). Sometimes we must continue praying, knowing that God hears our desperate cries. Especially when praying for others' salvation, we must not lose heart when it seems hopeless. We are commanded to pray; therefore, we must continue.

During my hospital stay and recovery, my family was encouraged to know that friends were praying with peace, power, boldness and consistency. Neither I nor my family could ever express our gratitude for the ones who faithfully prayed. Because my mother was confident about others' diligence in prayer during these struggles, she knew that when she could pray no longer, one of our friends was praying in her stead. What a blessing to have friends who pray!

9

My Room

For the days following the surgery, I remained on the left and right ventricular assist machines (the mechanical heart) so that my blood would continue to circulate. My own heart would not function during this time. From Saturday, August 22nd, through to Wednesday, August 26th, no one knew if I or my heart would recover. During these days, my incision was left open (bandaged) in case I needed to receive an emergency heart transplant.

Since I was unaware during this time, I have gathered information from my mother and my former school, The Montgomery Academy. Joyce Sweatt, the Academy's secretary, kept an ongoing list of my progress for faculty and students to see. Ms. Sweatt reported that on August 24th, the right side of my heart was working after the support system had been removed that morning. At the bottom of the note she wrote: 'Right side working 50 % without help. Left side working 25 % with help. Did not operate today.' On August 25th, Ms. Sweatt wrote: 'Nine-thirty a.m. – No change. Procedure will be done at 2 p.m. today to take left side off system. It can go either way!' Finally on August 25th, Dr. Kirklin took me off the last artificial heart machine. While the assist machines had been keeping me alive, the doctors had to remove them within a certain time frame so that I would not become dependent on them for survival. Gradually, the doctors had been removing the machines since the day after surgery. Meanwhile, unbeknown to me, I remained on the emergency transplant list.

Doctors had warned my parents that since these machines were experimental, they might cause dangerous side-effects such as strokes or blood clots. Finally, when they dismantled the left assist machine (the last one) my heart could function very weakly on its own. However, removing the last machine resulted in a blood clot in my brain and a seizure. Dr. Crawford later explained to me that blood clots tend to form on the LVAD machines even if the patient receives heparin as a blood thinner. Subsequently, the clots break loose and can travel to the brain, resulting in a stroke. Since it was suspected from a physical exam, the stroke was confirmed by doctors through a CT scan of my brain.

I was then unconscious for another week or so and continued on a respirator. On August 26th, Ms. Sweatt informed individuals: '7.30 a.m. Things are better! Heart operating on its own. Worry – infection, etc.' Later, she wrote another note: '3p.m. The brain scan did not look good but doctor said that too could change. Otherwise, she is making a slow recovery.' Another note, on August 27th reported: 'Today Margaret's eyes followed her Dad when he walked around. However, they are still concerned about brain damage.' Thankfully, God protected me from knowing about these complications.

While I was 'out', on Friday, August 28th, the doctors sewed up my incision, which had been open since the surgery. On August 30th, one of my former teachers, R. B. Roberts, and his wife visited the hospital. Following the visit, Ms. Sweatt wrote, 'Responding, moving arms. All are encouraged but must wait and see.' When I finally awoke from all of these events, the left side of my body was paralyzed. In addition, I had a mild case of dyslexia and memory loss. In spite of the negatives, one positive event happened – I got my own room in the CICU on Wednesday, September 2nd. I guess they knew I would be at UAB Hospital for a while so they moved me into a cubicle with a television. The doctors encouraged my parents to bring a Walkman from home so that I could listen to my favorite tapes (of the late Christian musician Rich Mullins) while sleeping. The medical team hoped that noise from television and radio would stimulate my brain and help me regain memories or other brain capacities which might have been disturbed. Thankfully, I could be away from all of the rows and rows of beds with yellow bodies (from the iodine that they clean and prepare people with) and the horrible sounds of ventilating machines, being exposed to everyone who passed by.

When I awakened in my CICU room, I began asking for pens and paper so that I could write notes. My innate and untamable desire to communicate was not hampered by the respirator – I was motivated to write. I kept the scribbled pages that I wrote on September 2nd (the day I awakened) that say: 'Can I have a diet coke?' 'Can I use the toilet?' 'Where's Daddy?' 'Can I spend the night at my grandmother's?' and 'When is RUF?' The writing looks jumbled, and I had a hard time interpreting it. Many of the letters are reversed, and many of the words run on top of each other. It was obvious that I did not realize the extent of what had happened or exactly where I was. Because I kept using UAB's progress note-paper, my mother brought me one of those Magni-Doodle pads with the plastic pencil. I could write all that I wanted to, erase it and start over. I was frustrated at not being able to speak because of the tube in my throat.

It was at this time that I discovered that I had suffered a stroke. My left side was paralyzed, and my left leg was in constant pain. I could not sleep at night because of the intense, sharp pain. Sleeping in the hospital bed was not too comfortable, especially since I was not used to sleeping on my back. However, with daggers in my leg, even with a pillow between my legs, I was in distress. For several weeks, the doctors were not sure if I had permanent brain damage or if I would be able to use my left side again. My father was glad that I was alive, even if it meant that I would be restricted.

On September 3rd, the Montgomery Academy note read: 'Margaret is responding to questions asked by family and doctors. She has written a note asking about her job. Story: Her mother was singing to her and asked Margaret if she wanted her to continue and Margaret indicated (some way?) NO!!' It was also on this day that the doctors took off the ventilator and replaced it with a face mask, noting that I was still very weak. The following day they put the ventilator back on. Obviously, I was not able to think straight! It was on this day that I wanted to call Billy Joseph, my campus minister, to tell him that I would not be at RUF for a while because I had suffered a stroke. I also thought that the doctors were doing aerobics in the hallway. They must have been making a lot of noise, and I am sure that I had a headache (inferring from other jumbled notes I wrote expressing pain in my head). I must have associated loudness with aerobics, and I was convinced that their noise was due to high impact! When they made their rounds, I asked the doctors if they had been aerobicizing!

After I moved to the new CICU cubicle, my parents began to tape all of the 'Get Well' cards on the walls. When I was able to move to a regular room, these cards filled up a big bag. Whenever the doctors came into my CICU room, they would compliment me on the 'wall paper' and admire the creative 'get well' cards.

I wrote that I had a sore throat and a headache and that I needed a bath. It bothered me so much that my hair was dirty and unkempt. I do not think I have ever gone that many days without shampooing my hair! I also saw a cow attached to the end of my bed and kept writing 'cow' because I wanted to know where it came from. I had forgotten that Laura and Sara McReynolds (now Laura Smith and Sara Lee) brought it to me on Thursday night before the surgery. In addition, I was very disturbed because I needed to go to the bathroom and did not realize that I had a catheter. I wrote to the nurse, 'I need to go to the toilet. My mother said never go to the bathroom in bed!' Again, I asked my mother to bring me 100 stamps and stationery pieces so that I could write people. When she brought only a few stamps, rather than 100, I became very agitated. I had great plans of writing letters to friends and relatives while I was there.

Later, I had to re-learn to tell time. I could not remember which was the minute hand and which was the hour hand on the clock. I still prefer a digital watch! Furthermore, my room did not have any windows so I never knew if it was day or night. The nurses finally hung a wall calendar in my room so that I would know what day it was. One day, Bill and Emmie Smith came by to visit on their way to the Alabama football game at Legion Field. I thought that it was late at night and that the game was over when actually it had not started. I stayed in constant confusion. However, with all of the cards, stuffed animals and cows, this tiny cubicle became 'my room'.

Billy Joseph recalls visiting me with his wife: 'When Margaret finally was in the clear, Marian and I visited her in her room, covered in her favorite Cow motif. Cards, balloons, drawings everywhere and all seemed to relate to cows. Margaret was cheerful and alert and we talked for a short time. The Lord had brought her through in His miraculous power.'

Thus I waited for recovery in 'my room'.

10

Who Has The Key?

Initially, my parents were allowed to visit the CICU for only fifteen minutes five times each day. Later the rules became more relaxed when the hospital staff realized that I was not leaving in the near future. Throughout the time without visitors, I slept a lot and felt extremely lonely. Often, one of my main day-shift nurses, Virginia Hamel, would read the Bible to me. One theme that I clearly remember from the CICU was the search for 'the key.'

Day and night, the nurses would walk around asking each other, 'Who has the key?' referring to the narcotics closet key. It became a joke between me and nurses on my floor. One particular male nurse whom I had a huge crush on, would come in my room at 3 a.m. when I was wide awake and would send my assigned nurse away on break. This nurse and I would talk and laugh until the other nurse returned. On the Christmas after I left the hospital, he called at the crack of dawn to ask me if I had the key!

As I have reflected on 'the key' concept, I have realized that we, as believers, have the key. Just as my body needed medication to function during that time, so unbelievers desperately need peace with God and forgiveness from sin. My body was going to die unless someone who had the key unlocked the closet and brought medicine to me. As Steve Brown often says, 'Evangelism is just one beggar telling another beggar where he can find bread.' In my analogy, evangelism is taking the key, unlocking the gospel and allowing God to provide the balm of grace to a lost sinner's soul.

Not only do we have the key, but Jesus Christ is the only key to eternal life. 'For there is one God and one mediator between God and men,' according to 1 Timothy 2:5-6, 'the man Christ Jesus, who gave himself as a ransom for all men – the testimony given in its proper time.' He offers the free gift of eternal life to everyone who receives it by faith. He, however, is the only access, the only Key. 'I am the way and the truth and the life. No one comes to the Father except through me' (John 14:6). Jesus describes those who think they have been 'good enough' apart from Him: 'Not everyone who says to me, "Lord, Lord" will enter the kingdom of heaven, but only he who does the will of my Father who is in heaven. Many will say to me on that day, "Lord, Lord did we not prophesy in your name and in your name drive out demons and perform many miracles?" Then I will tell them plainly, "I never knew you. Away from me, you evildoers!"'

(Matt. 7:21-23). It is not enough to just look like Christians, going through the motions – we must be transformed by His grace and His Spirit.

Not only is He our key, but also He is our Cornerstone, our Anchor. 1 Peter 2:4 describes our Lord Jesus Christ: 'As you come to him, the living Stone – rejected by men but chosen by God and precious to him – you also, like living stones, are being built into a spiritual house to be a holy priesthood, offering spiritual sacrifices acceptable to God through Jesus Christ.'

As our Key, Jesus promises never to leave us, never to forsake us. When we encounter the most difficult times in our lives, He will be there. Isaiah 43:1-3 tells us: 'Fear not, for I have redeemed you; I have summoned you by name; you are mine. When you pass through the waters, I will be with you; and when you pass through the rivers, they will not sweep over you. When you walk through the fire, you will not be burned; the flames will not set you ablaze. For I am the LORD, your God, the Holy One of Israel, your Savior.' Before the Israelites crossed over into the Promised Land, Moses delivered God's promise to them: 'Do not be afraid or terrified because of them, for the LORD your God goes with you; he will never leave you nor forsake you' (Deut. 31:6). Most likely, they had anxieties. They were losing their leader, Moses, whom God would not let into the Promised Land. They were gaining a new leader, a new land, a lot of unknowns. Even through the uncertainties, God reminded them that He would be with them.

The Lord promises to be with us in our earthly situations and unknown futures. He also promises to keep us throughout eternity. Before the crucifixion, He said to His disciples: 'Do not let your hearts be troubled. Trust in God; trust also in me. In my Father's house are many rooms; if it were not so, I would have told you. I am going there to prepare a place for you. And if I go and prepare a place for you, I will come back and take you to be with me that you also may be where I am' (John 14:1-3). He promises that we will dwell with Him and with the Father forever. Jesus truly is the Key and the Gatekeeper of eternity.

He is the Love that will not let me go.

O love that will not let me go,
I rest my weary soul in Thee;
I give Thee back the life I owe,
That in the ocean depths its flow
May richer, fuller be.

O cross that liftest up my head,
I dare not ask to fly from Thee;
I lay in dust life's glory dead,
And from the ground there blossoms red
Life that shall endless be.[9]

Since then we have the Key, Christians are called to evangelism, taking the Key to unbelievers. In addition to calling us out of the darkness and into the light, Jesus summons His disciples: 'Come, follow me, and I will make you fishers of men' (Matt. 4:19). Later in Matthew, Jesus commands, 'Therefore go and make disciples of all nations, baptizing them in the name of the Father and of the Son and of the Holy Spirit, and teaching them to obey everything I have commanded you' (Matt. 28:19-20). As our inalienable responsibility, believers must proclaim the Good News to the world.

What is evangelism? Evangelism is 'presenting Christ Jesus and His work in relation to the needs of fallen men and women, who are without God as a Father and under the wrath of God as a Judge. Evangelism means presenting Christ to them as their only hope, in this world or the next.'[10] While God is sovereign and does not 'need us,' He chooses to use us in accomplishing His purposes. We are ambassadors of Christ, heralds of truth, along with the apostle Paul.

How does God's sovereignty affect our evangelism? While God's sovereignty apparently seems to contradict man's responsibility in evangelism, both are a reality. God is all powerful, all-knowing, and it is He who saves. We are commanded, however, to proclaim the truth. Rather than causing us to become inactive in evangelism, God's sovereignty should motivate us. God's sovereignty does not allow us to guess which person God may want to save and thus act accordingly. Neither does it affect the urgency of the message or the genuineness of the Good News. On the contrary, we have boldness because of His sovereignty. As Romans clearly describes: 'I am not ashamed of the gospel, because it is the power of God for the salvation of everyone who believes: first for the Jew, then for the Gentile' (Rom. 1:16). We do not have to pressure ourselves with phrases such as 'the blood will be on me if this person rejects the gospel.' Such statements are not true. Those whom God has called, He will save, regardless of whether we present an effective message or an incoherent one.

Further, God's sovereignty moves us to be patient. Many missionaries have gone overseas and spent their entire lifetime without ever seeing one converted soul. However, they have faithfully planted seeds which others may later water and watch blossom. We can be patient when our unbelieving loved ones still have not received Christ as Savior because we know God is in control. And, His sovereignty leads us to prayer.

What are our motivations for evangelism? Our impetus for evangelism is two-fold – love for God and love for our neighbor. We are commanded to evangelize. Thus, as Jesus reminds, 'If anyone loves me, he will obey my teaching' (John 14:23). When asked about the greatest commandments, Jesus said, 'The second is like it: "Love your neighbor as yourself" ' (Matt. 22:39). Love for those around us motivates us to tell them the Good News. As Paul wonders: 'And how can they hear without someone preaching to them?' (Rom. 10:14). 'Our job, then, is to go to our fellow-men and tell them the gospel of Christ, and try by every means to make it clear to them; to remove as best we can any difficulties that they may find in it, to impress them with its seriousness, and to urge them to respond to it.'[11] When we love others, we will tell them about the hope for eternal life through Christ.

Why then are we not sharing the gospel? The answer is selfishness. Our condition is best described in the parable of the talents: 'Again, it will be like a man going on a journey, who called his servants and entrusted his property to them. To one he gave five talents of money, to another two talents, and to another one talent, each according to his ability. Then he went on his journey' (Matt. 25:14). The servants with five and two multiplied their talents, but the servant with one hid his talent. When the master returned, he rewarded the first two servants. However, the master was upset with the third servant, calling him lazy and wicked. The master took this servant's one talent away and threw the man outside. Christians have been given the key. We may use the excuses like 'evangelism is not my gift' or 'I'm doing relational evangelism.'

Describing relational evangelism, Metzger states: 'Relational evangelism, in spite of its good intentions, does not put its emphasis on hearing the word of truth as necessary kindling which the Holy Spirit ignites in regeneration. Relational evangelism's approach can neglect the theological content of the gospel...'[12] Often we begin forming friendships with non-Christians, but we never get around to sharing the gospel with them. If we are honest with ourselves, we fear being rejected by men more than we care for lost souls.

How do we then practically evangelize? While there are many pamphlets, seminars and plans on evangelism, I do not claim to be an expert on these specifics. However, I know that we are called to pray for unbelievers. In addition, we may gear our conversations away from chit chat and toward personal values and beliefs. With many unbelievers we encounter, we allow the conversation to revolve around the weather, football scores or shopping trends. Instead, we must ask people the tough questions which reveal their positions before God. Years later, working as a mental health counselor, I asked one of my clients (a teenager) about his artwork, which included sketches of the 'grim reaper' and Satan. Consequently I asked him if he knew for sure what would happen if he died on that day. One probing question opened up a way for me to present the gospel to this hurting soul. Our initial statements and questions do not have to be that direct, but we must lead conversations toward eternal matters.

What will be the result of evangelism? We will be reunited with people of all nations and tribes. As Revelation 5:9-10 explains: 'because you [Christ] were slain, and with your blood you purchased men for God from every tribe and language and people and nation. You have made them to be a kingdom and priests to serve our God, and they will reign on the earth.' The result of our evangelism will be that we will reign forever in heaven with other believers.

Following the example of Paul, we are called to evangelize even our enemies. When Paul and Silas were in jail in Rome, they sang hymns and prayed. A violent earthquake erupted, and the prison was shaken. Frightened, the jailer asked, 'Sirs, what must I do to be saved?' (Acts 16:30). Paul and Silas told him to believe on Jesus and be saved. This jailer who had once held the believers captive returned as a changed man, inviting Paul and Silas to his home. Even Jesus offered grace to the thief on the cross. 'Jesus, remember me when you come into your kingdom' (Luke 23:42). As we share our faith, individuals will be saved. We are obligated to witness to those with whom we want to spend eternity – friends, loved ones. Furthermore, we are commanded to spread the gospel to lost souls. Unless they are saved, unbelievers will face eternal judgment and damnation, separation from God. 'Who will not fear you, O Lord, and bring glory to your name? For you alone are holy. All nations will come and worship before you, for your righteous acts have been revealed' (Rev. 15:4). We will actually see and spend eternity with those who hear the gospel and are saved.

11

There's a Fungus Among Us

During these days in the CICU, my fever was spiking. The first record of fever was reported by my mother on Tuesday, September 1st. On Friday, September 4th, my mother noted: 'Still with respirator, hanging in there, very weak, had to put ventilator back on, rough night, fever very high.' On Saturday, September 5th, Dr. Kirklin, my surgeon said, 'She's doing better this morning, but I am perplexed about the fever. It has been between 101 and 104 for ten days.' During this serious fever episode, Dr. Kirklin had gone to Chicago for a speaking engagement. However, he flew back early, September 4th, because he thought I was about to die.

One night I was covered in an ice bath to arrest the fever, and the resident, Dr. Raleigh, stayed with me throughout the entire night. On Tuesday, September 8th my mother recorded the following: 'Okay night, fever 100.8, sat up in chair before 9 a.m. visit, asleep at 9 a.m.' I started sitting in a chair (for the first time on September 8th) and gradually started walking around the unit with someone holding me on both sides. Notes continued to hang at Montgomery Academy as I remained in the hospital. Also on September 8th, the note read: 'Report from Wade Segrest [a former principal] – he visited with family over weekend. It appears that one day Margaret makes some progress and they are encouraged and then the next day she isn't doing so well. This was the case over the weekend. Bad news – Margaret had to be put back on respirator this weekend and also she is running a fever. Good things – she is writing notes to family.'

Finally, on Wednesday, September 9, the doctors discovered that I had a deadly blood fungus called *Candida albicans* which was causing the high fever. It is not uncommon for heart valve recipients to receive a heart valve contaminated by Candida. When this situation occurs, patients need a new homograff or heart valve. Thankfully, my new valve was not previously infected. According to Dr. Bourge, everyone has Candida in their body. However, following a major medical stressor, the immune system is lower and infection may occur. My mother also reminded me that I could have incurred Candida when doctors put in a central line (similar to an IV).

Symptoms of Candida fungus include fever, nausea and diarrhea, abdominal tenderness. In addition to those difficulties, I also had the infection in my mouth, referred to as thrush. My mother remembered that the nurses made me swallow disgusting medicine and that this thrush caused my mouth to hurt. It was already difficult for me to eat, drink and keep nourishment down. Candida seemed to complicate my improvement. In most cases, once Candida is detected, patients, as I did, must start medication intravenously.

On September 9th, my mother reported: 'Ventilator off 11:30 a.m., 1 p.m. still off, saw Dr. Kirklin, told us about fungus.' On that day, I began taking anti-fungal medicine called Amphotericin B, the only systemic antibiotic available at that time, through the IV. After I started taking this medicine, I began feeling better but was nauseated a lot. On the same day the Candida was discovered, I wrote a note to my mother and said, 'Did you know I almost died?' After she said, 'Yes,' I wrote, 'I'm glad I didn't.' Even though I was gaining consciousness, I was still not 'out of the woods'.

On September 11th, the Montgomery Academy note said: 'She's off the respirator and they've figured out what's causing the fever. She's alert but weak.' Another note added: 'She is talking.' On Saturday, September 12th, I got to take a shower (while sitting on a chair of course). What a relief! Later on that same day however, my fever went back up to 103 and 104 degrees. On Sunday September 13th, my mother reported that I walked around the unit twice in the morning and once in the afternoon and went back to the shower. I enjoyed showering and shampooing my hair so much that I went as often as allowed! The physical therapists had begun walking with me around the unit until I was able to go to the physical therapy wing in a wheelchair.

On Monday, September 14th, I walked two times around the unit, was still nauseous and was sleeping at 10:30 a.m. The following day my mother wrote: 'Bad night, fever up, still tired and still nauseous.' On Wednesday, September 16th my mother noted: 'Felt better, walked three times around unit, rode stationary bike, fever still up during Tuesday night.' On Friday, September 18th, I had a 'terrible, horrible, no good, very bad day' and almost died. The Montgomery Academy note must have been written before this traumatic incident because it said: 'September 18th, Good News!! Margaret is 'walking, talking and chewing gum. All is well. Guitar practice will work out problems with left hand.' As I began to recover, I asked my father to bring my guitar from home so that I could practice. When Dad finally brought my guitar, I simply looked at it as if it were a foreign object. I could not remember any of the chords. I was pretty discouraged.

On this 'bad day,' September 18th, I went

downstairs with my nurse, Virginia Hamel, for a CAT scan. I remember feeling as if I needed to go to the bathroom very badly and trying to wait. Then I went into a cold room where I entered a tunnel (the CAT scan) and finally just wet the bed (or at least I thought I was wetting the bed). In the meantime, a tube going into my bloodstream fell out, my blood began falling onto the floor and I began to turn blue. I could not yell because the tunnel was making loud noises. When I came out of the tunnel, the nurse, Virginia, started screaming and telling someone to get oxygen immediately because I was bleeding to death. The whole thing shocked me, to say the least!

Meanwhile, as I was in the hospital, my best friend, Margaret Lois Phelps Romanowski, was due to be married on September 19th, the day after the 'bad day'. I kept thinking that I would be able to leave the hospital for the wedding and come back. One of the reasons I had scheduled the surgery for August 21st was so that I would be able to be involved with Margaret Lois's wedding. Dr. Kirklin had assumed that I would be out of the hospital around August 28th and soon back to work in Tuscaloosa. I knew that a month would be plenty of time to be home for the wedding. Margaret Lois and I had shared all kinds of adventures together: dating boys in

Ozark, Alabama; stealing a dog and taking it to Prattville to another one of Margaret Lois's beaus (as my grandmother would say); driving the car before we were sixteen – I did not want to miss this wedding. We were the female 'Tom Sawyer and Huck Finn' of our neighborhood, terrorizing younger siblings, cutting up in youth group and Sunday school! We had been through every major life event together, running to and from each other's house, sneaking in when one was on restriction. I was planning on being in Margaret Lois's wedding. Barring unforeseen complications, I had expected to be out of the hospital within the week of surgery.

However, I was so disappointed when the day arrived and the doctors did not let me leave. I really kept thinking that I would be able to make it and did not understand why I could not just 'check out' like at a hotel and come back to the hospital after the wedding. As mentioned previously, my thinking was skewed. A week before the wedding, I wrote Margaret Lois a letter and told her that I was coming even if I had to come in a wheelchair.

Here are excerpts from my letter to Margaret Lois, written September 12th: 'I hope to be in the wedding. Please don't give up on me. It means so much! They have to send me to a regular room outside of ICU (intensive care) first and make sure I can walk and breathe and eat. I know you won't believe it but I have no appetite.... One day, five doctors and nurses came in to put me in a chair and I had on NOTHING. It was terrible. They're keeping me filled with drugs, x-rays, breathing tests and much more. Oh well, it's just to get better which is what I hope for. I miss you a lot and will call you when I get home, hopefully one day this week.' Needless to say, I missed her wedding and remained in the hospital another month after writing the letter.

According to my mother, my progress improved on the following days. On Sunday, September 20th, I went to the chapel service at the hospital in a wheelchair and continued to attend each Sunday after that, gradually becoming able to walk to the chapel. On September 22nd, after I had started eating a little regular food, I began craving frozen yogurt. It had been one of my staple foods before the surgery. On that day I was able to walk to the hospital cafeteria and eat chocolate yogurt, which did not taste very good after all – too sweet! It was quite an adventure, and I enjoyed getting out of the CICU. After these days, I really do not have a daily record of my progress. As I began improving, I guess my mother stopped keeping notes.

Eventually, about a week before my first discharge from the hospital (on October 6th), I moved to a room on the regular cardiac floor. I continued to recover there, but I did not get much rest. Every morning at 4 a.m. a lady smacking chewing gum would walk in and turn all of the lights on and ask me to get out of bed to weigh. My mother finally asked this nurse if she could come a little later, as I have never been a 'morning person'. In addition, my parents arranged to have different sitters stay with me at night because I was still too weak to get up by myself if I needed to go to the bathroom or anything. I had the IV pole that had to go with me wherever I went, and it was difficult for a healthy person to maneuver.

My mother wrote down my daily hospital schedule after I moved to the regular room:

6:00 a.m.	pills
8:00-8:30	breakfast
9:00-10:00	Occupational therapy
10:00-11:30	Rest
12:30	Lunch
1:00-2:30	Rest (one pill at 2:00)
2:45-4:00	Physical Therapy
4:00	Pills
4:15	Rest

As you can see, my days were not too thrilling!

When my brother William was out of college for Fall break, he came to see me. He was sitting in the room with me while Mom was taking a break or going to get a soft drink. I was sound asleep until I felt something touching my skin in my shirt. I nearly jumped out of the bed as I saw a suspicious-looking male nurse whose name tag was crumpled and worn. I was horrified that he would 'check the I.V.' while I was sound asleep. My brother thought I was crazy and insisted that the unknown man was a legitimate employee, but I had seen television programs (like Dateline) about people pretending to be nurses. Eventually, it became a funny story in our family. My mother went to the nurses' station to make sure that he was really a nurse, which he was; and she told him to wake me up before any more procedures. We all had to keep some humor during this time!

12

Patience for the Impatient Patient

By nature I am not a very patient person! Because my recovery was slow, I had no other choice but patience. The doctors ordered Physical Therapy on my left leg before I was even conscious so that I would not lose muscle tone. While I was in the coma, the physical therapists began bending my legs and left foot. It was obvious to the medical staff that I had a stroke because my left foot was drooping. So they began my very slow process toward recovery.

Occupational Therapy began soon after I regained consciousness, working with my left hand which was very weak. I could not grip a glass in that hand, and I had forgotten how to button shirts and tie shoes. To help me learn how to dress myself once again, my mother bought me a 'Dressy Bessy' doll (like the one I had as a child). Bessy had buttons, shoe laces, snaps and other accessories. I felt that I truly had reverted to childhood with my Dressy Bessy and Magni-Doodle! In addition to playing with my toys, I attended Occupational Therapy daily. At OT I used my left hand to squeeze modeling clay and put rubber bands over nails on a board. I also picked up pegs and put them into holes. Because the tasks in OT were difficult and painful, I hated OT and was easily frustrated with it. One day I told them I was never coming back, so they did not come and get me the following day. When I told my mother that I was not returning, she became very upset and angry with me. She called OT and apologized. From that point on, I had no choice but to go – pain or no pain!

In Physical Therapy I walked a lot, rode a stationary bicycle, and walked up and down a set of stairs on the physical therapy wing. I enjoyed PT because it was a challenge. Setting new goals each week, I saw progress in accomplishing them. Once I returned home, the doctors told me to continue walking and riding the bicycle. At first, however, I was so weak that I could not walk to the end of my parents' driveway and back. Gradually I worked up to walking for an hour (four years later).

Reflecting on these slow steps toward recovery, I am reminded that our culture is not used to slow progress. There are laws against speeding because it is our nature to hurry, even if we endanger others' lives. As a matter of fact, patience is an anomaly in our culture, as is other-worldliness. We are used to having fast food, microwave ovens, ATM machines, express oil change, and instant grits. For me to have a slow recovery of physical strength was an adjustment and a challenge. I expected to be back to normal quickly, while it actually has taken years. When my husband, Bill, played football in high school, he hurt his arm. The doctor told him not to play for several weeks. However, Bill thought he was okay and decided to play in the game that week. Much to his surprise, Bill broke his leg. While the fracture was below the knee, the same doctor who had given specific instructions the previous week put Bill in a cast up to his hip 'to teach him a lesson'. Even though that story is a humorous one to me, it illustrates how often we are 'forced' to learn patience in difficult ways.

What is patience? Webster's Dictionary defines patience as 'enduring pain, trouble or confusion without complaining.' To examine this concept further, we must note that patience is one of the attributes of God. Scripture interchanges the terms patience, long-suffering and slow to anger. As Nahum 1:3 describes patience: 'The LORD is slow to anger and great in power.' 'The Hebrew uses the expression *'erek'aph*, which means literally, "long of face",' writes Louis Berkhof in *Systematic Theology*.[13] Rather than destroying the wicked in an instant, the Lord waits for their repentance.

In *The Attributes of God*, A. W. Pink further defines God's long-suffering, contrasting patience and mercy: 'It [patience] differs from mercy in the formal consideration of the object: mercy respects the creature as miserable, patience respects the creature as criminal; mercy pities him in his misery, and patience bears with the sin which engendered the misery, and is giving birth to more.'[14] Pink further explains that God's patience may be seen as His control over Himself, restraining Himself from giving the wicked what they deserve – immediate destruction.

In *The God You Can Know*, Dan DeHaan surmises that God's patience is often 'passed over without comment' because 'His perfection is far beyond our ability to comprehend it. We have clear limits in our understanding of patience.'[15] For forty years, the Lord showed patience to the Israelites who wandered, complaining, doubting. 'We all know that if we were in God's position, their murmuring would have brought us to our limit within the first of the forty years.'[16] Throughout the Old Testament, the Lord demonstrated patience toward His people. The prophets, sent by God, challenged the Israelites about their sinning against Him and reminded them that God was displeased with their attitudes and behaviors. These preachers asked 'why' and expressed God's woe, according to DeHaan.[17] Furthermore, they declared God's patience, called for repentance and lastly told of His wrath. 'We should be amazed that we suffer so little for the consequences of our sins. Entire nations spurn His name and nothing happens.... How patiently He bears our own depraved conduct.'[18] We marvel at His slowness to anger.

Paul expounds on God's patience in Romans 9: 'What if God, choosing to show his wrath and make his power known, bore with great patience the objects of his wrath – prepared for destruction? What if he did this to make the riches of his glory known to the objects of his mercy, whom he prepared in advance for glory – even us whom he also called...' (vv. 22-24). The Lord's patience declares His goodness and grace. We also see patience in the life of the Lord Jesus who constantly showed patience to His disciples: 'You see nothing but unchanging pity, compassion, kindness, gentleness, patience, long-suffering and love. He does not cast them out for their stupidity.'[19] The patient God writes long-suffering onto the hearts of His children.

Patience is one of the fruits of the Spirit. According to Galatians 5:22-23: 'But the fruit of the Spirit is love, joy, peace, patience, kindness, goodness, faithfulness, gentleness and self-control. Against such things there is no law.' We are called to be clothed with patience: 'Therefore, as God's chosen people, holy and dearly loved, clothe yourselves with compassion, kindness, humility, gentleness and patience' (Col. 3:12). This passage continues, encouraging believers to forgive those who have wronged them and to be bound in love. As Christ has shown immeasurable patience toward us, we must be patient with one another. 1 Peter 3 reminds us of Noah's time: '...when God waited patiently in the days of Noah while the ark was being built. In it only a few people, eight in all, were saved' (3:20). When we recall God's patience with us, we are motivated to bear with one another.

Believers are commanded to be patient as we wait on the Lord. According to James 5: 'Be patient, then, brothers, until the Lord's coming. See how the farmer waits for the land to yield its valuable crop and how patient he is for the autumn and spring rains. You too, be patient and stand firm, because the Lord's coming is near' (vv. 7-8). Christians will show patience in the following areas: with one another, in suffering and in anticipating the Lord's return.

Before I left the hospital the first time (October 6th), I had to go back to the operating room in order for the doctors to insert a Groshong catheter in my chest (so that I could continue taking medicine by IV when I was at home). I was very frightened! I did not understand what was happening to me. As they wheeled me off, I was crying hysterically, and I continually recited the twenty-third Psalm. Although I associated the operating room with trauma, pain and complications, I was reminded that my Father is my Shepherd who looks after me. And at that time, the twenty-third Psalm was the only Scripture I could remember.

Even in my distress, I was comforted by thinking of the patient Shepherd. The first three words, 'The Lord is,' represent the Old Testament equivalent of 'I am who I am'. This phrase, 'I am' indicates that God is unchanging and almighty! Following those three words appears a contrast, 'my shepherd,' which in Israel 'was considered the lowest of all works.'[20] The Lord God Almighty who declared His name to Moses in the burning bush defines Himself as our Shepherd, a lowly occupation.

From what I understand about sheep, they are not too intelligent. In fact, they are prone to wander off and are easily afraid. Because of the peculiarities of sheep, the one responsible for them must be 'long-suffering'. As James Boice describes: 'Shepherds had to live with the sheep twenty-four hours a day, and the task of caring for them was unending. Day and night, summer and winter, in fair weather and foul, they labored to nourish, guide, and protect the sheep.'[21] R.C. Sproul notes that 'The ancient shepherd was armed. He would use the crook of his staff to rescue a fallen lamb from a pit. He would wield his rod against hostile beasts that sought to devour his sheep...as long as the shepherd was present the lamb had nothing to fear.'[22] David knew from first hand experience what patience this task required.

Jesus told a parable about a lost sheep: 'Suppose one of you has a hundred sheep and loses one of them. Does he not leave the ninety-nine in the open country and go after the lost sheep until he finds it? And when he finds it, he joyfully puts it on his shoulders and goes home' (Luke 15:4-6). The shepherd seeks after the one lone sheep and guides it safely home. Then he calls his friends together to rejoice over finding this lost sheep. Our Shepherd not only regenerates our hearts, but He rejoices over our restoration.

Jesus describes Himself as the Shepherd: 'I am the good shepherd; I know my sheep and my sheep know me – just as the Father knows me and I know the Father – and I lay down my life for the sheep' (John 10:14-15). Sproul further says about our Lord: 'But we have a Shepherd who cannot fall. We have a Shepherd who cannot die. He is no hireling who abandons his flock at the first sign of trouble. Our Shepherd is armed with omnipotent force.'[23] As our Shepherd, Jesus consistently guides, protects and even dies for us.

On another occasion, I had to have a blood

transfusion. Either the need for the transfusion was urgent (not enough time for family members to donate blood) or I did not have a family member with the same blood type. I do not remember. However, I became obsessed with the idea that I would contract the AIDS virus through someone else's blood. I became very discouraged and wondered if I had the strength to continue fighting for life. My thinking was distorted, and my mother explained that I became 'fixated' on ideas, having a hard time getting false thinking out of my mind. Because of my stroke, I was easily bewildered. I thought, 'With the way things are going, I'll probably contract AIDS through this transfusion.' However, I forced myself to remember that my Shepherd was leading me. Thankfully, I used my Walkman and listened to Rich Mullins' rendition of this wonderful hymn when I felt afraid and alone.

All the way my Savior leads me;
What have I to ask beside?
Can I doubt His tender mercy,
Who through life has been my Guide?
Heavenly peace, divinest comfort,
Here by faith in Him to dwell!
For I know whate'er befall me,
Jesus doeth all things well.

All the way my Savior leads me,
Cheers each winding path I tread,
Gives me grace for every trial,
Feeds me with the living bread.
Though my weary steps may falter,
And my soul athirst may be,
Gushing from the Rock before me,
Lo! a spring of joy I see.

All the way my Savior leads me;
Oh, the fullness of His love!
Perfect rest to me is promised
In my Father's house above.
When my spirit, clothed immortal,
Wings its flight to realms of day,
This my song through endless ages:
Jesus led me all the way.

(Fanny Crosby)

13

Yuck-the Scar

When I first looked at my chest and saw the stitches, I saw a bunch of black spider-legs and was extremely grossed out. I had only needed stitches one other time in my life, and those were on the back of my head where I could not see them without two mirrors. Now my body had been cut in half, and stitches were all I could see! For a long time I was afraid to touch my scar or even to look at it very much. As a matter of fact, I did not touch it until several weeks out of the hospital. I looked in the mirror and said, 'This is not me. This is not my body.' Horrified at the swollen, red, crookedly cut malformation, I concluded that I was a freak!

One of the reasons that my scar looks so grotesque is that my incision was open for a week. Usually heart patients refer to their scars as 'zippers' because they eventually fade into a thin white line. Mine, however, is still crooked, bumpy, very wide and obvious. I used to try and cover the top part with Dermablend, a makeup for malformations or scars. I was self-conscious, not wanting to wear any shirt or dress that revealed this distortion. For a while, I must have looked like a Victorian woman with collars up to my chin. Later, I became adjusted to my mark and now I do not even notice it.

As I have pondered this scar over the years, I have finally concluded that it is my mark. My scar is like a birth mark because it distinguishes my body and stands out. It is actually a grace-mark. Because it is a sign that God wanted to give me extra days on this earth, it is a mark of Grace. He was not ready for me to depart and be with Him. For some reason, He chose to let me stay around; and He left a mark on my body signifying His decision. As Paul describes: 'For to me, to live is Christ and to die is gain' (Phil. 1:21). Only when I finally returned to my parents' house did I realize the seriousness of what had happened to me. I continued to face the possibility of heart transplantation (and may one day need this surgery). My 'routine' aortic valve replacement surgery had backfired; to me, a heart transplant seemed the equivalent of death.

As I became comfortable with my new body and this grace mark, I struggled with questions about my future. 'Will any man be able to love and accept me with this distorted body?' 'Will I ever go on another date?' At first I was embarrassed to wear a bathing suit because I believed that the scar stuck out so obviously. I clung to Isaiah 54:5: 'For your Maker is your husband – the LORD Almighty is his name – the Holy One of Israel is your Redeemer; he is called the God of all the earth.' I had no one to trust in except for Christ. He became my Everything.

Before August 1992, I would have intellectually agreed that I would be willing and ready to suffer for Christ, as stated by Paul: 'I want to know Christ and the power of his resurrection and the fellowship of sharing in his sufferings, becoming like him in his death, and so, somehow, to attain to the resurrection from the dead' (Phil. 3:10-11). Since my surgery, however, I have more vividly understood that God is glorified when we participate in Christ's sufferings.

In the Old Testament, God made a covenant with the Israelites. As part of the covenant, the Israelites had specific ways in which they could worship the Lord. Their sacrificial system, involving animals, was a foreshadowing of Christ's coming to earth to die for our sins. They understood that blood must be shed as payment for their sins. Even though their worship service involved sacrifices, the Israelites were saved, as we are, by trusting in the promised Messiah. As Ryle describes: 'It was Christ who was the substance of the ceremonial law which God gave to Israel by the hand of Moses. The morning and evening sacrifice, the continual shedding of blood, the altar, the mercy-seat, the high priest, the Passover, the day of atonement, the scapegoat – all these were so many pictures, types, and emblems of Christ and His work.'[24]

When Jesus came to earth as the God-Man, the Messiah, He became the Sacrificial Lamb. John the Baptist proclaimed: 'Look, the Lamb of God, who takes away the sin of the world!' (John 1:29). Just as the Israelites who placed blood over their doorposts were spared from losing their firstborn, so believers marked with the Lamb's blood will escape judgment. As 1 Corinthians 5:7 states: 'For Christ, our Passover lamb, has been sacrificed.' Jesus was the fulfilment of Isaiah 53:7: 'He was oppressed and afflicted, yet he did not open his mouth; he was led like a lamb to the slaughter, and as a sheep before her shearers is silent, so he did not open his mouth.' Again, he was 'pierced for our transgressions, he was crushed for our iniquities' (Isa. 53:5). We cannot even begin to conceive of the suffering Christ endured on our behalf. However, when we endure hardships, somehow we join in His suffering.

As I searched for additional explanations of my condition, I stumbled onto Hezekiah's story. I read about Hezekiah's illness in 2 Kings and then in the prophecy of Isaiah. I empathized with Hezekiah who was told to put his house in order because he was going to die. 'Remember, O LORD, how I have walked before you faithfully and with wholehearted devotion and have done what is good in your eyes,' he prayed. 'And Hezekiah wept bitterly' (Isa. 38:3). The Lord showed favor to Hezekiah and extended his years. 'Then the word of the LORD came to Isaiah: "Go and tell Hezekiah, This is what the LORD, the God of your father David, says: I have heard your prayer and seen your tears; I will add fifteen years to your life"' (Isa. 38:4-5). Later in the same chapter are reflections Hezekiah made following his illness and recovery.

Hezekiah expressed some of the same emotions I felt and asked similar questions. 'I said, "In the prime of my life must I go through the gates of death and be robbed of the rest of my years?...I am troubled; O Lord, come to my aid!" But what can I say? He has spoken to me, and he himself has done this. I will walk humbly all my years because of this anguish of my soul.... Surely it was for my benefit that I suffered such anguish. In your love you kept me from the pit of destruction; you have put all my sins behind your back' (Isa. 38:10, 14-15, 17). I began praying Hezekiah's prayer – that the Lord would extend my days.

At the same time, I began truly longing for heaven. I remember the Thanksgiving following my surgery. As I sat at the dinner table at my parents' home, I felt as if I was there but not there. I was viewing the scene from another perspective, as if I were not present. While I felt a tinge of sorrow, I longed for my eternal home with Christ. I had a similar feeling to what Paul expressed to the Philippians: 'I am torn between the two: I desire to depart and be with Christ, which is better by far,' states Paul, 'but it is more necessary for you that I remain in the body. Convinced of this, I know I will remain, and I will continue with all of you for your progress and joy in the faith' (Phil. 1:23-25). As a result of these life events, I began to see life from both an earthly and eternal perspective (one eye on heaven and one on earth).

My 'job' in the hospital was fairly easy. However, my struggles intensified when I returned home. While I was in the hospital, I enjoyed seeing friends and family members; when I returned home, my mother told people not to visit for a while. For days and weeks, I sat in the den or rested in my bed, isolated, alone. Where was God during this time? I could barely walk half way down the driveway and would turn around to find that I was so exhausted I could only go back to bed. All the while, I felt as if everyone else's life had gone on. I was stuck, just like a child, depending on my mother to help me into the bathroom. I had to ask for her help because I had the 'pole' for IVs to drag along with me. Furthermore, my mother had to help me take showers. She bought a bench and placed it in the shower since I was too weak to stand up.

Aside from loneliness and physical limitations, I struggled with my own anger and grief, feeling as if God was going to cut my life 'short'. I had dreamed of getting married. Now I wondered if I would ever go on another date. I desperately clung to Jesus as my Rock, my comfort through this storm. Second Corinthians 1:3-4 describes our comfort: 'Praise be to the God and Father of our Lord Jesus Christ, the Father of compassion and the God of all comfort, who comforts us in all our troubles, so that we can comfort those in any trouble with the comfort we ourselves have received from God.' Those of us who face storms and live may be able to comfort others at a later date. God is glorified when we suffer, persevere and consequently minister grace to others.

From an RUF newsletter written October 28th 1992:

Dear Friends:
While in UAB Hospital, I received a gift of a teddy bear. He looks very old and rejected with his matted hair and sad, black eyes. He looks worn out, but actually he's soft and cuddly

with a real mushy stomach. I like to talk to him (which is crazy). One night I said he was cute and precious and that I loved him. All of a sudden I realized that my view of Teddy is like God's view of me. He loves me so much that He died for me and He saved me from death most recently. God knows exactly how He made us and He loves us in spite of ourselves.

As you know, I was in the hospital about six weeks with open-heart surgery, which led to a stroke, a seizure and heart failure, and then they found a blood infection called Candida.

As of October 6, I am at home recovering and still taking medicine to kill the infection. I have a semi-permanent catheter which allows me to take the medicine intravenously. I am growing stronger every day, am able to walk outside, but still have a long way to go.

I'd like to share with you something I wrote in my journal on August 18 before the surgery:

Each day the surgery is more a reality. Had a strange sensation tonight, looking around my room, that I could die. Yes, it's possible. I'm not so much worried about myself as my parents. They would have to be strong and know it's the Lord's perfect will. I've got a lot more living I'd like to do – marriage, kids, ministry. I've come to appreciate life. But some people have a clock inside that ticks and stops too soon – like Sandy Ford (Leighton Ford's son).

What would happen if I died? I would pass instantly into fellowship with my Lord Jesus Christ. I hope loved ones left behind would celebrate my home-going and look forward to their joining me.

Again, I cannot thank you enough for all the prayers and thoughts. At the hospital they call me 'Miracle Margaret' because they have never seen anyone in my condition recover! God still does miracles and answers prayers – I understand this fact much more now. I realize how much He loves those with matted hair, rejected and lonely. Think of Teddy.

Love in God's goodness,
Margaret

One day when God creates a new heaven and a new earth, my body will be restored to perfection. The only One who will have a scar will be Jesus. Peter writes: 'For you know that it was not with perishable things such as silver or gold that you were redeemed from the empty way of life handed down to you from your forefathers, but with the precious blood of Christ, a lamb without blemish or defect' (1 Peter 1:18-19). He will continue to have nail-scarred hands and probably a scar on His side – His real Grace marks. 'Doubting Thomas' wanted to see the scars before he would believe that the others had seen the Lord. 'Unless I see the nail marks in his hands and put my finger where the nails were, and put my hand into his side, I will not believe it.' Several days later, Thomas was able to see Jesus and feel His scars. When he did he said to Jesus: 'My Lord and my God!' (John 20:25, 28). While we may have accumulated scars and 'battle wounds' in this life, the Lamb will continually bear His marks.

As Paul writes: 'Therefore I will boast all the more gladly about my weaknesses, so that Christ's power may rest on me. That is why, for Christ's sake, I delight in weaknesses, in insults, in hardships, in persecutions, in difficulties. For when I am weak, then I am strong' (2 Cor. 12:9-10). Would that we all delighted in these troubles! Just as we have participated in His sufferings, we will praise Him eternally. Revelation 5:6 presents a picture of what awaits believers: 'Then I saw a Lamb, looking as if it had been slain.' In heaven we will have a visible reminder of Christ's scars. Then, John records the scene: 'In a loud voice they sang: "Worthy is the Lamb, who was slain, to receive power and wealth and wisdom and strength and honor and glory and praise!"' (Rev. 5:12). We will never forget the pain that

He endured for our sakes when all of our scars
have vanished. Every knee will bow and every
tongue confess that Jesus Christ is Lord.

> See, from his head, his hands, his feet,
> Sorrow and love flow mingled down:
> Did e'er such love and sorrow meet,
> Or thorns compose so rich a crown?
>
> (Isaac Watts).

14

My Return to UAB

On October 6th, I returned to my own house and room following so many weeks of trauma. However, I was unable to keep any solid foods in my system because I was still taking the Amphotericin B (referred to as Amphi-Terrible due to its side effects) at home each night. Dr. Kirklin had sent me home with a Groshong catheter, through which a home health nurse could come and connect the medicine that would continue to fight the deadly blood fungus. In addition, he placed me on several other medications (in pill form) that would regulate my heartbeat and prevent nausea. I was overjoyed to see my own room and to just be there.

The Amphotericin B was so strong and potent that my hair began falling out and I was nauseated twenty-four hours a day. Furthermore, my teeth constantly chattered, even if the temperature was eighty degrees. I could not drink a glass of water without vomiting. When I had nothing in my system to throw up, I coughed up phlegm. And every time I tried to swallow a pill, I choked on it and threw up more.

Word traveled quickly around Montgomery

that I was home and nauseated. Thus, many people brought special dishes for me to try. They would come to the door, speak briefly with my mother, and leave. Some of the unique foods I remember trying were baked custard, apricot juice and frozen Italian ice. Unfortunately, I could not keep them down. Even though I could not eat, individuals kept bringing the food. My father told me that he gained a lot of weight by eating these dishes in hopes of encouraging me to eat!

On October 13th, one week later, I had to return to see Dr. Kirklin for my check up. Although I tried to act as if I was feeling fine, Dr. Bourge (my follow-up cardiologist) and Dr. Kirklin knew better. The blood tests showed that my electrolytes were out of balance. Thus, they asked me to come back to the CICU at the hospital. They originally thought that if I went home and ate food that my mother fixed I would be able to get rid of the nausea and gain strength. However, they did not know that my mother had forgotten how to cook! Not really – I threw up all of the good food that she tried to feed me. I spent one night in the CICU and then went back to the regular cardiac floor. I tried to eat foods for a week, starting on a liquid diet of soups and jello and finally advancing to meat. The doctors also gave me an anti-fungal pill, Diflucan, that I could swallow. Finally, I would be rid of the IV and the Amphotericin B. The entire arrangement was a lot easier on my system. And I began taking a potassium pill that was easier to swallow. The previous one was the size of my mouth. Before I could swallow it, the potassium would dissolve in my mouth, making me vomit because it tasted so disgusting.

With a new way to take potassium and a different anti-fungal drug I began eating again. The doctors also took me off another medication which had become toxic in my blood. The last night at the hospital I ate a gourmet chicken dish (from the VIP wing of the hospital) and kept it down! I was set to go home again! I returned to Thomas Avenue in Montgomery for the second time on October 20th.

15

Outsiders Look In

In this chapter I want to mention some thoughts about this experience as seen through the eyes of others (some who knew me personally and some who did not). An RUF student previously quoted, John Hunter, told me that he learned a lot about God's sovereignty during my illness: 'I understand myself better, that I must value Christ alone.' The body is secondary, and believers should not hold onto it. 'When a crisis occurs, God is on top of any crisis. We ought to let the crisis happen, not asking why,' explained John. 'We ought to ask how we can be an instrument through our difficulties.'

Cynthia Whisnant, one of the hospital chaplains, asked if she could use my story in one of her sermons, of which I share an excerpt:

(Speaking on the text of Hosea 11:1-11) – The same is true of Hosea as he speaks of a consumed people, scheming, devoured, enslaved. And the despair may touch our insides in a way we cannot name, the disappointments we've known as parent, as child, as creation of God. We may feel trapped, enslaved, wondering all the while if love still works its wonders in us. Take heart today. I've someone I want you to meet in addition to Hosea. Her name is Margaret, and Margaret, along with Hosea, has something to teach us about a love too strong.

Margaret entered the hospital a few weeks ago, a woman in her early twenties facing cardiovascular surgery. I did not know her then. I learned of her during surgery and listened as her parents were told that a routine procedure had exploded with cardiac complications. Margaret's condition was worse than initially envisioned. I knew it was bad when the surgeon acknowledged that they were doing all that they could surgically, but this would be determined by the hands of God. As the hours passed, I learned more about Margaret. Her reputation preceded her. I was amazed at the number of staff persons who knew her through family and friends. I was amazed at the number of friends and friends of friends who waited on Margaret – not to mention family. And I listened to the stories of the wonderful, faithful person she is.

Margaret came down from surgery with nearly every assist device (machine) imaginable. Most everyone used their skills, held their breath, hoped, prayed and waited on Margaret – for many days. Margaret lives today and I count her as a miracle. The machines have been removed and though she's not out of the forest yet, the deepest, darkest woods are behind her. Lately, Margaret has been pointing to Scriptures, literally, that have been on her mind. One she has been thinking on is from Isaiah 40:11: 'He tends his flock like a shepherd: He gathers the lambs in his arms and carries them close to his heart . . .'

With her permission, I have shared Margaret's story with you today. If I compare Margaret's life with this Hosea text, I believe she must have been nurtured and loved by God as a child, surrounded by human kindness, bent down to and fed. Her Bible, with its markings, her parents, give evidence to that. She embodies to me faithfulness to God and by God. And though I do not believe Margaret's complications were due to sinfulness or punishment, I do believe God intervened and used her survival as a lesson for sometimes faithless, confused and often struggling people. God is still faithful. God is still God and can work even through machines. For Margaret's story portrays to me a different kind of love.

Here is a song written by Susan Welch – former

Clemson University RUF student whom I have never met. I quote it here with permission.

Margaret's Song

Sometimes I think we live with blinders on
and soon we forget that life is not so long
but if we could see our lives when time has come
                                              and gone
I wonder what we'd choose to place importance on

Chorus:
Will what you do be here when life is through
will all that you say last longer than today
and will everything you're living for
lead someone else to heaven's door
or will it burn away like stubble, wood, and hay
will it be here tomorrow or only last for today?

And let us not forget about our words
which when shared with wisdom can be priceless
                                        when they're heard
and let us not withhold them and look back with regret
wondering what could have been if they had just been
                                                    said
    Chorus

Life won't be all it could be unless it lasts through time
and spoken words can travel but our silence stays behind
think how sweet 'twould be to stand before His face
and see the footsteps of our lives lead others to His grace
    Chorus

Here is a letter, written on October 13th, 1992, from one of the individuals who received my RUF newsletters:

Dear Mark Lowrey (RUF Coordinator at that time)

Thank you for your beautiful letter in which you enclosed the newsletter which Margaret Carroll wrote before entering the hospital! What an inspiration and testimony her faith – and life – has been to us all. We continue to pray for her strength and healing – and her invincible spirit in serving her Lord.

Another card, written in September 1993:

Dear Margaret,
...all that you are doing sounds so great. Keep up the good work. I love the news that you are writing a book. Be sure to include our method of prayer for you each day!* Yes, we all want a copy! ...We shall continue to pray

* This note was written by Joyce Sweatt, secretary at my former school, The Montgomery Academy. Their method of prayer was to place notes and drawings of me on the teachers' mailboxes each day. If I had a good day, the writing and drawings would be very big; but if it was a 'bad' day, she would write with tiny letters. Her wonderful notes and drawings kept faculty and students aware of how I was doing and how they could specifically pray.

for your improvement. Thank goodness you are getting better constantly.

From The RUF at Alabama RUF NOTES:

Volume 1, Number 1 – Margaret Carroll Needs You

Alabama RUF intern Margaret Carroll, who is approaching her fourth week in UAB Hospital's CICU, needs to know we are praying for her and thinking about her as she slowly recovers from her heart surgery and all of the serious complications that accompanied it. Please correspond to Margaret by sending your cards and letters to . . .

RUF NOTES Volume 1, Number 2 – Margaret: Homeward Bound??

It's more than just a rumor that 'MeeMaw' * might whisper from her rocker. It's a reality! As you read this bulletin, Margaret is crawling into her own bed for the first time in nearly seven weeks, having survived more trauma within that span than most of us will suffer in a lifetime. Margaret will be under 'house arrest' in Montgomery for several more weeks as she continues to recover. Please do not cease

---

* Some students called me 'MeeMaw' because I could do wonderful impersonations of my grandmother!

your prayers for her. Her condition is still physically sensitive. She will continue to receive IV medications for her infection during the p.m. hours, and Margaret still has a lot of strength to be regained. Visitation, especially for the next week, will be limited. Send her 'Welcome Home' cards, and thank God for the mighty work He has done.

RUF NOTES from October 20 1992 – What's afoot at the Carroll Corral

Alabama RUF intern and heart surgery survivor, Margaret Carroll, appears to finally be back home in Montgomery for good after her return trip to UAB Hospital last week due to nausea and dehydration. As it turns out, a toxic level of a particular medication being administered was the cause of her setback. Today, Margaret ate a real meal for the first time since August 21. Who ever thought chicken-pot pie could be a sentimental experience? Margaret also put together an outline today for a book she will be writing about the whole experience and about the visible movement of God she and others have witnessed.

Looking back at these RUF Note excerpts, it seems that the writer had a good sense of humor in trying to describe my condition and progress to fellow college students. I could continue placing notes, letters and cards in this chapter, as many individuals wrote to me during this time. However, I would like to add thoughts of individuals who were around me through this experience and recovery.

Jerdone Davis, the female RUF staff person at Clemson, reflected on my hospital stay:

'I remember coming into cardiac ICU to see you after you had the little stroke. You were limp as a kitten and not moving anything. I don't think you were even aware at that point of anything going on. You were on life support (if I remember correctly). My nursing judgment was that you would not make it! Your wounds were packed at that time and covered with huge bandages – in other words, your chest was wide open to heal. Prayers were going up for you all over anywhere that I knew about. It seemed I would hear every day of someone on the other side of the world who was praying for your healing!!! Shirley was in Australia and they were praying for you in the Presbyterian churches there.

'I remember the spurts of excitement we would all experience by phone as Mark would update us on your progress. I learned so much about the **ejection** factor and how weak your heart was. You were very faithful to do everything that the doctor told you to do and your heart increased very slowly in strength over the next few years. Every time there was a phone call about you, there was a reason to praise God and celebrate over His healing touches on you! What a thrilling and awesome experience to be "in on" His definite work on your behalf!

'Oh yeah! I remember the James 5 service you requested of the campus ministers. How sweet that was to have each of them lay hands on you and pray for your healing! I remember the privilege it was for me and Jean Lappin to be there praying as the ministers gathered around you. What an awesome night!!'

Virginia Hamel, one of my day shift nurses, reminded me that I became very depressed while in the hospital. She encouraged me to be patient and courageous through the difficult circumstances.

Billy Joseph, RUF campus minister, also reflected:

'It is very difficult for me to remember specifics of those events. Even as I think back on the whole episode of Margaret's heart surgery and recovery I am still lost in a sea of disconnected memories. There are many memories, but how they connect to each other, I cannot remember. Are the memories disconnected because of my feeble ability to remember or because of the overwhelming number of things that happened? I am not sure.

'As a campus minister the most difficult memory is formed because I don't deal with death that much. It is a reality on the college campus but most often it is sudden with little time for thinking or preparation. There are always weddings, dating relationships etc. but death isn't a common, everyday problem on campus. Neither is a sickness as serious as Margaret's condition a common, everyday occurrence. If a student gets that sick, usually they are home quickly and the help I offer is from a distance. The campus is a sheltered community with death and sickness as infrequent visitors.

'The presence of Margaret's upcoming surgery therefore raised concerns only among the students to whom Margaret was close. The average student only knew that Margaret was going to have surgery but not what kind. The students Margaret had specifically ministered to formed the core of those who I kept informed as the situation progressed from surgery to life and death struggle. Their close connection to her meant that they needed to be informed about as much as possible, but also encouraged and comforted by me in Margaret's absence.

'Many students were open to Margaret after the ordeal. Her suffering and recovery clearly demonstrated God's grace and power and this was evident to the students. They could not get away from the facts that God had worked a miracle in her life.

'The ordeal also gave Margaret a sense of urgency in dealing with people. She understood what life was about and that it was precious and short. She was able to get past the subterfuge that people place in the way of the gospel and move them to confront the real issues of life.'

When the body of Christ surrounds a hurting soul, amazing things happen. As 1 Corinthians 12 describes: 'If one part suffers, every part suffers with it; if one part is honored, every part rejoices with it. Now you are the body of Christ, and each one of you is a part of it' (12:26-27). As the old saying goes, there is strength in numbers. My mother told me that while I was in the hospital, she often would become discouraged. During those weeks, Mom and Dad would spend the night at my aunt and uncle's house in Birmingham, and then Dad would drive to Montgomery the following morning for work. On several occasions, my Uncle Ben and Aunt Pat went out of town, so my mother was alone during the day. She would drive to the hospital to see me, but I was often asleep when she arrived. On some days she would hear good news from the nurses in the morning and then bad news at the afternoon visit.

Most of the time, my mother felt exhausted. She told me that the body of Christ helped sustain her. On one occasion, she did not feel as if she could read the Bible, so she found a Steve Brown tape I had ordered (it came that day in the mail). On other occasions, friends would call just when she needed to hear an encouraging word.

16

Home Free

For several years following the surgery, I continued to have regular check-ups with Dr. Robert Bourge who is now my cardiologist. I returned to Tuscaloosa to work with RUF in January 1993; however, I found myself unable to do as much as I had before the surgery because I was frail. During one of my visits with Dr. Bourge in 1993, he told me that my heart was very weak and that I still might need a heart transplant. Dr. Bourge wanted to wait for one year, hoping that my heart would 'bounce back' from the surgery and complications. Apparently, the first year would be the crucial window of opportunity for the heart to recover. Dr. Bourge explained to me that the heart is like a rubber band – once it gets stretched past a certain point, it is harder for it to rebound.

I was scheduled to have a heart catheterization in August 1993, after spending the summer in Montgomery with my parents. This catheterization involved having a tube placed in the side of my neck and then into the heart. It would provide a clearer understanding of my heart's overall functioning and would determine my need for a transplant. Thus, I returned to the Kirklin Clinic (part of UAB) for this procedure. The doctors were surprised at the results of the heart catheterization, which showed that my heart was doing better than they expected. An echo-cardiogram had previously measured my heart's pumping at around 12%. While this percentage was low, my heart was not getting larger (which is common with a low pumping capacity).

The heart's ejection fraction, or pumping percentage, may be measured through several means: echocardiogram, muga (a test wherein dye is injected into one's bloodstream) or heart catheterization. Measuring the proportion of blood contained in and expelled from the ventricle, the ejection fraction indicates the heart's functioning. A normal person's ejection fraction is usually around 65%. Since the surgery, my ejection fraction had stayed between 12 and 15%. My diagnosis was congestive heart failure. According to Dr. Bourge, my chance of a full recovery with these percentages was less than 20%.

These low percentage numbers continued into the beginning of 1994. At that time, I still had to see Dr. Bourge quarterly, and I continued working with RUF at Alabama. Finally, at the RUF Summer Conference, out of desperation, I asked the campus ministers and staff to please pray for me and with me about my health. Almost every campus minister and many staff members met with me in one of the classroom buildings at Laguna Christian Beach Retreat and began praying, laying hands on me, confessing personal and corporate sins for several hours. Each of us trusted in God's promises concerning the prayer of faith from James 5:13-16:

'Is any one of you in trouble? He should pray. Is anyone happy? Let him sing songs of praise. Is any one of you sick? He should call the elders of the church to pray over him and anoint him with oil in the name of the Lord. And the prayer offered in faith will make the sick person well; the Lord will raise him up. If he has sinned, he will be forgiven. Therefore confess your sins to each other and pray for each other so that you may be healed. The prayer of a righteous man is powerful and effective.'

On my next visit to the Kirklin Clinic, several weeks later in May, the heart's pumping had improved to 17%. The doctors, who had given up hope of any improvement after the first year, were amazed that my heart's pumping was beginning to increase after almost two years. After the October visit with Dr. Bourge, here's the fax that I sent to all of the RUF campus ministers and staff:

To Campus Ministers and Staff:
I am writing to thank you for your prayers and encouragement over the past two years regarding my health. I'd like to update you on the ways in which God is healing me physically, pertaining to my most recent doctor's visit on October 20, 1994. Both the nuclear and echocardiogram tests showed that my 'heart has remarkably improved,' according to Dr. Bourge, my cardiologist. The pumping capacity or ejection fraction, has increased from 17% to 35-40% according to these results. While the tests detected overall improvement, they also revealed that the aortic valve (the one that was implanted) has worsened. It is leaking a 'little bit more' than before. Usually, Dr. Bourge explained, when the valve leaks, the heart may appear to be doing better but is at the same time getting enlarged. In my case the heart has decreased in size, 'almost back to a normal size.' When I asked how this could be, Dr. Bourge said, 'It's a miracle.'

Dr. Bourge thinks that he can control the valve leakage with medicine and said that this is the best condition in which he has ever seen my heart. Again, he could only explain that these changes occurred through prayer. 'Frankly, I can't believe it,' he said, earlier telling me that there was only a 1-2% chance it would ever get better. When I asked him about a transplant, he said, 'You don't need it.' I asked, 'Ever?' and he replied, 'Hope not.' Please continue to pray that my heart does not get larger, that the valve does not worsen and that the medicine will work!

I would like to thank you all for your prayers and especially for the awesome prayer time at Summer Conference. While I was praying and hoping for my condition to at least stay the same (to buy time for medical advancements) God has done exceedingly and abundantly far more than I could have imagined! The Lord continues to teach me numerous truths about Himself; and hopefully this update will encourage you in the power of prayer and of our God!

Love, Margaret

Even though my heart has improved beyond all odds, issues of life and death continue to be on my mind. Enduring such an experience has changed my entire perspective: 'Set your minds on things above, not on earthly things' (Col. 3:2). In addition, I realize that God did not have to heal me; I certainly did not deserve it. In Exodus 33 Moses wanted to see God's glory. The Lord responds; 'I will have mercy on whom I will have mercy, and I will have compassion on whom I will have compassion' (Ex. 33:19). The Lord alone chooses those to whom He will show favor and those whom He will heal.

As I have reflected on this life's fleeting nature, I have been forced to examine my own standing before God. Because He saved me, I have hope beyond this life. An encouragement for loved ones of believers is found in 1 Thessalonians 4:13-16: 'Brothers, we do not want you to be ignorant about those who fall asleep, or to grieve like the rest of men, who have no hope. We believe that Jesus died and rose again and so we believe that God will bring with Jesus those who have fallen asleep in him.... For the Lord himself will come down from heaven, with a loud command, with the voice of the archangel and with the trumpet call of God, and the dead in Christ will rise first.' What an amazing scene to imagine!

As J. C. Ryle describes: 'Christ will be all in heaven.... So in the same manner will Jesus fill the eyes of all who enter glory. In the midst of the throne, surrounded by adoring angels and saints, there will be "the Lamb that was slain"...the praise of the Lord Jesus will be the eternal song of all the inhabitants of heaven...the service of the Lord Jesus will be one eternal song of all. Blessed is the thought that we shall at length attend on Him without distraction, and work for Him without weariness. The presence of Christ Himself shall be one everlasting enjoyment of the inhabitants of heaven.'[25] One of the amazing aspects of heaven is that we will be free from sin. We will no longer have evil thoughts, greedy desires, lustful intentions and mixed motives. Our condition will be *non posse pecarre* – not possible to sin.

In addition to being free from sin, we will have no more sorrow, no sickness, no tears. Revelation 21 elaborates on our hope: 'Now the dwelling of God is with men, and he will live with them. They will be his people, and God himself will be with them and be their God. He will wipe every tear from their eyes. There will be no more death or mourning or crying or pain, for the old order of things has passed away' (vv. 3-4). This description of heaven makes my earthly pains more bearable, knowing that they are only temporary inconveniences.

The Westminster Shorter Catechism sums our future as follows in Question 38: 'What benefits do believers receive from Christ at the resurrection? At the resurrection, believers being raised up in glory, shall be openly acknowledged and acquitted in the day of judgment, and made perfectly blessed in the full enjoying of God to all eternity.' We have a marvelous hope for our future with Christ!

I wrote the following thoughts on October 19th, 1992, while still in the hospital:

You must wonder what I have learned:

1. That life, each day, every aspect, every breath and every heartbeat is a blessing.

2. I am unworthy – knowing my own inner self – to receive such grace from God.

3. What matters is not money, popularity, social prestige, house or car but a relationship with the Savior and with other people.

4. Because God's grace flowed so freely to me, it should naturally flow back out to other people from my heart.

5. That I am undeserving of anything that I have.

My heart has continued to strengthen over the years. I 'retired' from my work with RUF in 1995 to return to school. Since this time, I have married, finished a Masters Degree in Counseling and am working part-time as a Children's Therapist.

However, I still long for my permanent home. I realize that I am merely an alien on this earth: 'For here we do not have an enduring city, but we are looking for the city that is to come' (Heb. 13:14). While I am thankful for **friends**, health, blessings and salvation, I am always mindful that each day and breath are a gift. The Lord has already numbered our days; thus, a person's life is never 'cut short' for those who trust in God's sovereignty.

Recently, I read an article by R. C. Sproul entitled 'Death The Final Calling', which challenged me with the truth that dying is a vocation, a divine calling. 'Every one of us is called to die, and that vocation is as much a calling from God,' writes Sproul, 'as is a "call" to the ministry of Christ. Sometimes the call comes suddenly and without warning. Sometimes it comes with notification in advance. But it comes to us all. And it comes from God.' Sproul writes of this vocation: 'When God gives us a vocation to die, he sends us on a mission. We have indeed entered into a race...we wonder if we have the courage to make our way to the finish line, for the trial takes us through the valley of the shadow of death. It is a valley where the sun's rays often seem to be blotted out. We approach it trembling, preferring to seek a safe bypass.' Finally, Sproul encourages the believer: 'Even more important is His promise to guide us to what lies beyond. The valley of the shadow of death is not a box canyon, but a passageway to a better country.'[26] In that better country is the God of Abraham, Isaac, David – the God of the Living. One day I hope to say, with the apostle Paul, 'I have fought the good fight, I have finished the race, I have kept the faith' (2 Tim. 4:7). Thankfully, the Lord Jesus holds the keys to death. At His beckoning call, Death will be my summons by God in His divine sovereignty and timing.

As Christians, we cling to the promise of 1 Corinthians 15: 'When the perishable has been clothed with the imperishable, and the mortal with immortality, then the saying that is written will come true: "Death has been swallowed up in victory." "Where O death, is your victory? Where, O death, is your sting?"....But thanks be to God! He gives us victory through our Lord Jesus Christ' (vv. 54-55, 57). Death is victory for the Christian. When Jesus rose from the dead, He conquered death for His children. And He defeated Satan and his only power. When believers die, we reap the benefits of Christ's completed work on the cross.

Death still seems scary because it is unknown. No one that we have known in our lifetime has died and then returned to tell about it. The closest that I have come to death (besides my own surgery and recovery) was watching my maternal grandmother die. Her breathing became erratic, and then she made a coughing noise. She was gone. When I think of my own death, I do not like to imagine dying in a fire, in a car wreck or suffering a long, slow, painful death – as probably no one does. But when God ordained my birth and my days, He also ordained my death. It is not for me to choose when or how I will die. I must simply go when He calls.

Death is merely a doorway, a step into an eternity more amazing and beautiful (for believers) than our finite, self-centered minds can comprehend. One of the neatest songs I have ever heard is called 'We will dance one day.' When I heard it for the first time, I was unable to run, do aerobics, play basketball or tennis and other activities I so enjoy. The lyrics describe us as we will be one day and for eternity. Our bodies and souls will be united and made perfect to dwell with the Lord forever. We will all dance one day. What a marvelous thought! Every Christian who has any kind of debilitating ailment or limitation will one day be able to dance and never get tired or face shortness of breath.

Not only will I no longer break out with acne (yes, my face still looks like a pimpled teenager), but I will no longer struggle with sin. I will not have evil, jealous thoughts, covetousness, selfish motives and nasty pride. I will be righteous! As described in *The Westminster Confession of Faith*:

> The bodies of men, after death, return to dust, and see corruption: but their souls, which neither die nor sleep, having an immortal subsistence, immediately return to God who gave them. The souls of the righteous being made perfect in holiness, are received into the highest heavens, where they behold the face of God, in light and glory, waiting for the full redemption of their bodies (Ch 32, section 1).

On that last day our restored bodies will be reunited with our souls forever to know joy in the Lord's presence.

Knowing my future hope, I wrestle with this body of sin. Paul describes my condition in 2 Corinthians 5:2, 6-8:

> Meanwhile we groan, longing to be clothed with our heavenly dwelling, because when we are clothed, we will not be found naked.... Therefore we are always confident and know that as long as we are at home in the body we are away from the Lord. We live by faith, not by sight. We are confident, I say, and would prefer to be away from the body and at home with the Lord.'

Part of a Puritan prayer further expresses our future:

> Here I am an ant, and as I view a nest of ants
> so dost thou view me and my fellow-creatures;
> But as an ant knows not me, my nature, my
> thoughts, so here I cannot know thee clearly,
> But there I shall be near thee, dwell with thy
> family, stand in thy presence chamber, be an
> heir of thy kingdom, as the spouse of Christ,
> as a member of his body, one with him who is
> one with thee, and exercise all my powers of
> body and soul in the enjoyment of thee...as I
> hope to praise thee eternally hereafter.[27]

One day I will be at home, my eternal home. There I hope to see you as I run marathons on the golden streets. Be sure and wave and say hello as I race by!

From *The Heidelberg Catechism*, a question and answer of great hope:

> Question one: What is your only comfort, in
> life and in death?

> That I belong – body and soul, in life and in
> death – not to myself but to my faithful Savior,
> Jesus Christ, who at the cost of his own blood
> has fully paid for all my sins and has
> completely freed me from the dominion of the
> devil; that he protects me so well that without

the will of my Father in heaven not a hair can fall from my head; indeed, that everything must fit his purpose for my salvation. Therefore, by his Holy Spirit, he also assures me of eternal life, and makes me wholeheartedly willing and ready from now on to live for him.

Only one life will soon be past; only what's done for Christ will last.

17

Conclusion

My closing prayer from *The Valley of Vision,* a book of Puritan prayers:

Lord, High and Holy, Meek and Lowly,
Thou has brought me to the valley of vision,
where I live in the depths but see thee in the
heights;
hemmed in by mountains of sin I behold thy
glory.

Let me learn by paradox
that the way down is the way up,
that to be low is to be high,
that the broken heart is the healed heart,
that the contrite spirit is the rejoicing spirit,
that the repenting soul is the victorious soul,
that to have nothing is to possess all,
that to bear the cross is to wear the crown,
that to give is to receive,
that the valley is the place of vision.
Lord, in the daytime, stars can be seen from
deepest wells,
and the deeper the wells the brighter thy stars
shine;

Let me find thy light in my darkness,
thy life in my death,
thy joy in my sorrow,
thy grace in my sin,
thy riches in my poverty,
thy glory in my valley.

Bibliography

Bennett, Arthur, *The Valley of Vision*, The Banner of Truth Trust, Carlisle, Pennsylvania, 1975.

Berkhof, Louis, *Systematic Theology*, Eerdmans Publishing Company, Grand Rapids, Michigan, 1991.

Boice, James Montgomery, *Psalms*, Vol. 1, Baker Books, Grand Rapids, Michigan, 1994.

DeHaan, Dan, *The God You Can Know*, Moody Press, Chicago, Illinois, 1982.

The Heidelberg Catechism, 400th Anniversary Edition, United Church Press, Cleveland, Ohio, 1962.

The Holy Bible, New International Version, Zondervan Bible Publishers, Grand Rapids, Michigan, 1973.

Lloyd-Jones, D. Martyn, *Spiritual Depression*, Erdmans Publishing Company, Grand Rapids, Michigan, 1965.

Metzger, Will, *Tell the Truth*, InterVarsity Press, Downers Grove, Illinois, 1984.

Packer, J. I., *Evangelism and the Sovereignty of God*, InterVarsity Press, Downers Grove, Illinois, 1961.

Packer, J. I., *Knowing God*, InterVarsity Press, Downers Grove, Illinois, 1973.

Pink, A. W., *The Attributes of God*, Baker Book House, Grand Rapids, Michigan, 1975.

Ryle, J. C., *Holiness*, Evangelical Press, Durham, England, 1979.

Sproul, R. C., 'Death the Final Calling', *Modern Reformation*, Vol. 8, no. 3, pp. 34-37, 1999.

The Trinity Hymnal, Great Commission Publications, Suwanee, Ga, 1990.

The Westminster Confession of Faith, together with *The Larger Catechism* and *The Shorter Catechism*, Christian Education and Publications of the PCA, 1990.

References

1. Anonymous, *Trinity Hymnal*, Great Commission Publications, Suwanee, Ga, 1990, p. 466
2. 1. Some of these are taken from Josh McDowell's book, *His Image, My Image*, pp. 100-101.
3. J.C. Ryle, p. 193.
4. D. Martyn Lloyd-Jones, p.221
5. J. I. Packer, *Knowing God*, p. 236.
6. J. I. Packer, *Knowing God*, p. 150.
7. D. Martyn Lloyd-Jones, p. 228.
8. J.C. Ryle, p. 194.
9. George Matheson, Trinity Hymnal, p. 708.
10. J. I. Packer, *Evangelism and the Sovereignty of God*, p. 39.
11. J. I. Packer, *Evangelism and the Sovereignty of God*, pp. 92-93.
12. Metzger, p, 109.
13. Louis Berkhof, p. 72.
14. A. W. Pink, p. 62.
15. Dan DeHaan, p. 55.
16. Dan DeHaan, p. 56.
17. Dan DeHaan, p. 56.
18. Dan DeHaan, p. 56.
19. J.C. Ryle, p. 205.
20. James Montgomery Boice, p. 207.
21. James Montgomery Boice, pp. 207-8.
22. R.C. Sproul, p. 36.
23. R.C. Sproul, p. 36.
24. J.C. Ryle, p. 304.

25. J.C. Ryle, p. 311.
26. R.C. Sproul, pp. 34, 36, 37.
27. Arthur Bennett. p. 204.

Christian Focus Publications publishes biblically-accurate books for adults and children. The books in the adult range are published in three imprints.

Christian Heritage contains classic writings from the past.

Christian Focus contains popular works including biographies, commentaries, doctrine, and Christian living.

Mentor focuses on books written at a level suitable for Bible College and seminary students, pastors, and others; the imprint includes commentaries, doctrinal studies, examination of current issues, and church history.

For a free catalogue of all our titles, please write to
Christian Focus Publications,
Geanies House, Fearn,
Ross-shire, IV20 1TW, Great Britain

For details of our titles visit us on our web site
http://www.christianfocus.com